Collins
WORLDATLAS
bringing the world to life

GW00586948

contents

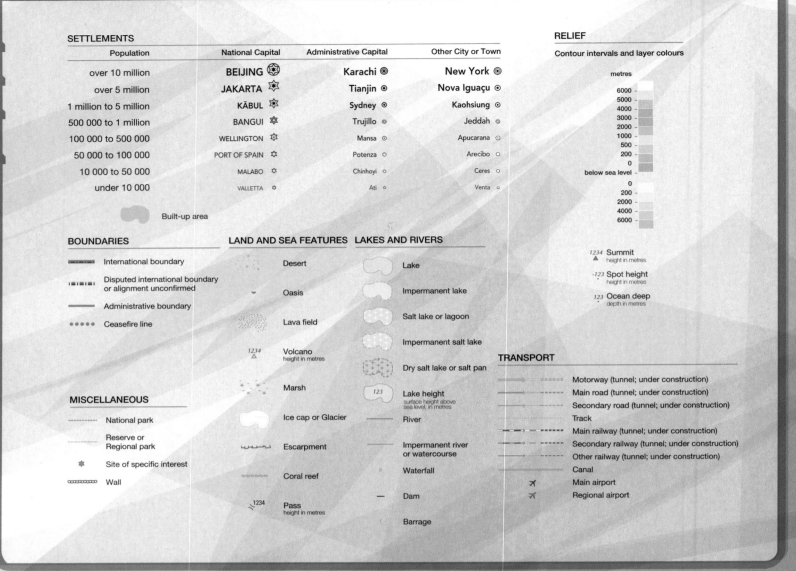

SETTLEMENTS

Population	National Capital	Administrative Capital	Other City or Town
over 10 million	BEIJING	Karachi	New York
over 5 million	JAKARTA	Tianjin	Nova Iguaçu
1 million to 5 million	KĀBUL	Sydney	Kaohsiung
500 000 to 1 million	BANGUI	Trujillo	Jeddah
100 000 to 500 000	WELLINGTON	Mansa	Apucarana
50 000 to 100 000	PORT OF SPAIN	Potenza	Arecibo
10 000 to 50 000	MALABO	Chinhoyi	Ceres
under 10 000	VALLETTA	Ati	Venta

Built-up area

RELIEF

Contour intervals and layer colours

metres

6000
5000
4000
3000
2000
1000
500
200
0
below sea level
0
200
2000
4000
6000

1234 Summit
height in metres

-123 Spot height
height in metres

123 Ocean deep
depth in metres

BOUNDARIES

- International boundary
- Disputed international boundary or alignment unconfirmed
- Administrative boundary
- Ceasefire line

LAND AND SEA FEATURES

- Desert
- Oasis
- Lava field
- 1234 Volcano
  height in metres
- Marsh
- Ice cap or Glacier
- Escarpment
- Coral reef
- 1234 Pass
  height in metres

LAKES AND RIVERS

- Lake
- Impermanent lake
- Salt lake or lagoon
- Impermanent salt lake
- Dry salt lake or salt pan
- 123 Lake height
  surface height above sea level, in metres
- River
- Impermanent river or watercourse
- Waterfall
- Dam
- Barrage

MISCELLANEOUS

- National park
- Reserve or Regional park
- Site of specific interest
- Wall

TRANSPORT

- Motorway (tunnel; under construction)
- Main road (tunnel; under construction)
- Secondary road (tunnel; under construction)
- Track
- Main railway (tunnel; under construction)
- Secondary railway (tunnel; under construction)
- Other railway (tunnel; under construction)
- Canal
- Main airport
- Regional airport

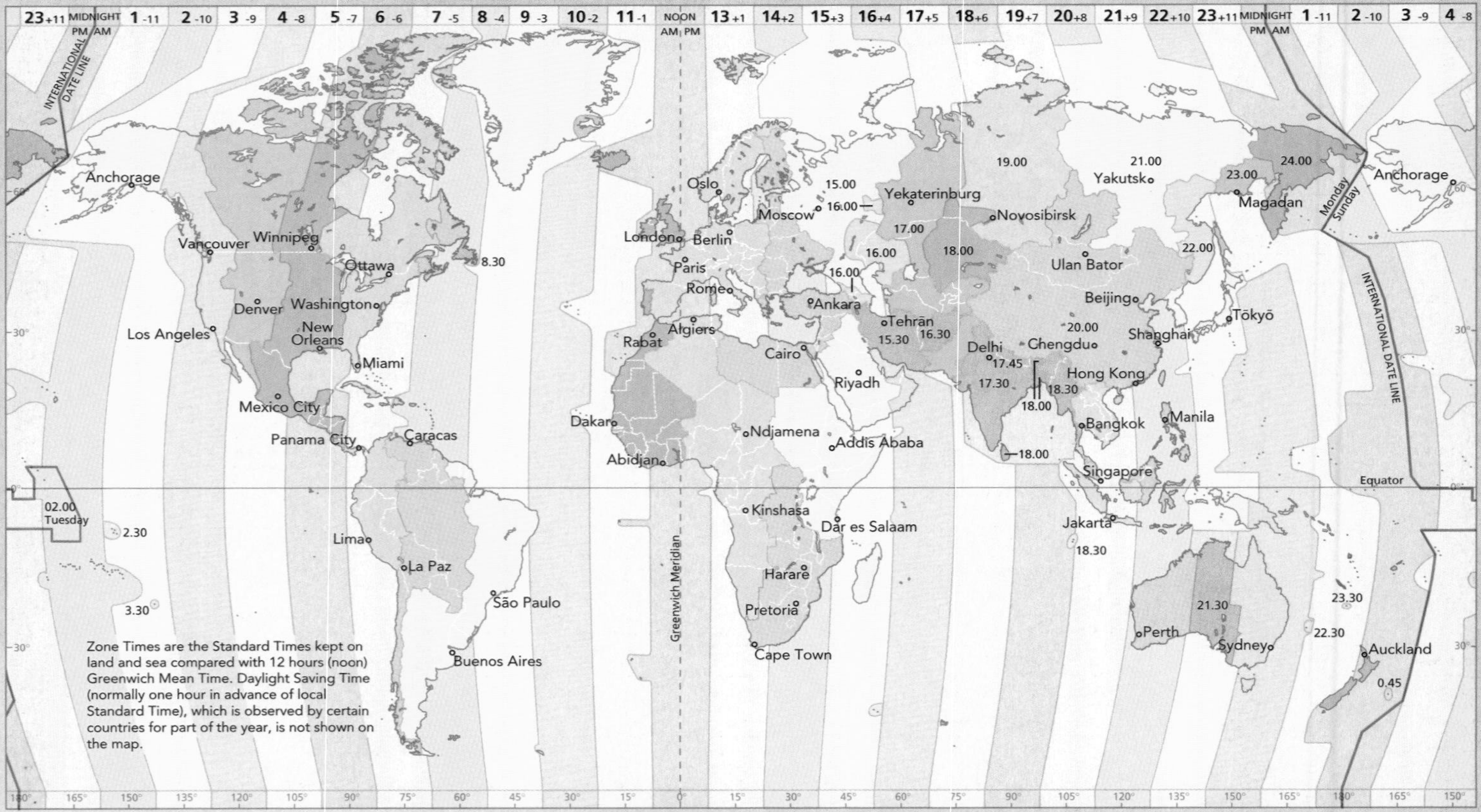

Zone Times are the Standard Times kept on land and sea compared with 12 hours (noon) Greenwich Mean Time. Daylight Saving Time (normally one hour in advance of local Standard Time), which is observed by certain countries for part of the year, is not shown on the map.

EUROPE	area sq km	area sq miles	population	capital	languages	religions	currency
ALBANIA	28 748	11 100	3 164 000	Tirana	Albanian, Greek	Sunni Muslim, Albanian Orthodox, Roman Catholic	Lek
ANDORRA	465	180	94 000	Andorra la Vella	Spanish, Catalan, French	Roman Catholic	Euro
AUSTRIA	83 855	32 377	8 069 000	Vienna	German, Croatian, Turkish	Roman Catholic, Protestant	Euro
BELARUS	207 600	80 155	10 106 000	Minsk	Belorussian, Russian	Belorussian Orthodox, Roman Catholic	Belarus rouble
BELGIUM	30 520	11 784	10 276 000	Brussels	Dutch (Flemish), French (Walloon), German	Roman Catholic, Protestant	Euro
BOSNIA-HERZEGOVINA	51 130	19 741	4 126 000	Sarajevo	Bosnian, Serbian, Croatian	Sunni Muslim, Serbian Orthodox, Roman Catholic, Protestant	Marka
BULGARIA	110 994	42 855	7 790 000	Sofia	Bulgarian, Turkish, Romany, Macedonian	Bulgarian Orthodox, Sunni Muslim	Lev
CROATIA	56 538	21 829	4 657 000	Zagreb	Croatian, Serbian	Roman Catholic, Serbian Orthodox, Sunni Muslim	Kuna
CZECH REPUBLIC	78 864	30 450	10 250 000	Prague	Czech, Moravian, Slovak	Roman Catholic, Protestant	Czech koruna
DENMARK	43 075	16 631	5 343 000	Copenhagen	Danish	Protestant	Danish krone
ESTONIA	45 200	17 452	1 361 000	Tallinn	Estonian, Russian	Protestant, Estonian and Russian Orthodox	Kroon
FINLAND	338 145	130 559	5 183 000	Helsinki	Finnish, Swedish	Protestant, Greek Orthodox	Euro
FRANCE	543 965	210 026	59 670 000	Paris	French, Arabic	Roman Catholic, Protestant, Sunni Muslim	Euro
GERMANY	357 028	137 849	81 990 000	Berlin	German, Turkish	Protestant, Roman Catholic	Euro
GREECE	131 957	50 949	10 631 000	Athens	Greek	Greek Orthodox, Sunni Muslim	Euro
HUNGARY	93 030	35 919	9 867 000	Budapest	Hungarian	Roman Catholic, Protestant	Forint
ICELAND	102 820	39 699	283 000	Reykjavík	Icelandic	Protestant	Icelandic króna
IRELAND, REPUBLIC OF	70 282	27 136	3 878 000	Dublin	English, Irish	Roman Catholic, Protestant	Euro
ITALY	301 245	116 311	57 449 000	Rome	Italian	Roman Catholic	Euro
LATVIA	63 700	24 595	2 392 000	Riga	Latvian, Russian	Protestant, Roman Catholic, Russian Orthodox	Lats
LIECHTENSTEIN	160	62	33 000	Vaduz	German	Roman Catholic, Protestant	Swiss franc
LITHUANIA	65 200	25 174	3 682 000	Vilnius	Lithuanian, Russian, Polish	Roman Catholic, Protestant, Russian Orthodox	Litas
LUXEMBOURG	2 586	998	448 000	Luxembourg	Letzeburgish, German, French	Roman Catholic	Euro
MACEDONIA (F.Y.R.O.M.)	25 713	9 928	2 051 000	Skopje	Macedonian, Albanian, Turkish	Macedonian Orthodox, Sunni Muslim	Macedonian denar
MALTA	316	122	393 000	Valletta	Maltese, English	Roman Catholic	Maltese lira
MOLDOVA	33 700	13 012	4 273 000	Chişinău	Romanian, Ukrainian, Gagauz, Russian	Romanian Orthodox, Russian Orthodox	Moldovan leu
MONACO	2	1	34 000	Monaco-Ville	French, Monegasque, Italian	Roman Catholic	Euro
NETHERLANDS	41 526	16 033	15 990 000	Amsterdam/The Hague	Dutch, Frisian	Roman Catholic, Protestant, Sunni Muslim	Euro
NORWAY	323 878	125 050	4 505 000	Oslo	Norwegian	Protestant, Roman Catholic	Norwegian krone
POLAND	312 683	120 728	38 542 000	Warsaw	Polish, German	Roman Catholic, Polish Orthodox	Złoty
PORTUGAL	88 940	34 340	10 049 000	Lisbon	Portuguese	Roman Catholic, Protestant	Euro
ROMANIA	237 500	91 699	22 332 000	Bucharest	Romanian, Hungarian	Romanian Orthodox, Protestant, Roman Catholic	Romanian leu
RUSSIAN FEDERATION	17 075 400	6 592 849	143 752 000	Moscow	Russian, Tatar, Ukrainian, local languages	Russian Orthodox, Sunni Muslim, Protestant	Russian rouble
SAN MARINO	61	24	27 000	San Marino	Italian	Roman Catholic	Euro
SERBIA AND MONTENEGRO	102 173	39 449	10 522 000	Belgrade	Serbian, Albanian, Hungarian	Serbian Orthodox, Montenegrin Orthodox, Sunni Muslim	Dinar, Euro
SLOVAKIA	49 035	18 933	5 408 000	Bratislava	Slovak, Hungarian, Czech	Roman Catholic, Protestant, Orthodox	Slovakian koruna
SLOVENIA	20 251	7 819	1 983 000	Ljubljana	Slovene, Croatian, Serbian	Roman Catholic, Protestant	Tólar
SPAIN	504 782	194 897	39 924 000	Madrid	Castilian, Catalan, Galician, Basque	Roman Catholic	Euro
SWEDEN	449 964	173 732	8 823 000	Stockholm	Swedish	Protestant, Roman Catholic	Swedish krona
SWITZERLAND	41 293	15 943	7 167 000	Bern	German, French, Italian, Romansch	Roman Catholic, Protestant	Swiss franc
UKRAINE	603 700	233 090	48 652 000	Kiev	Ukrainian, Russian	Ukrainian Orthodox, Ukrainian Catholic, Roman Catholic	Hryvnia
UNITED KINGDOM	244 082	94 241	59 657 000	London	English, Welsh, Gaelic	Protestant, Roman Catholic, Muslim	Pound sterling
VATICAN CITY	0.5	0.2	472	Vatican City	Italian	Roman Catholic	Euro

ASIA	area sq km	area sq miles	population	capital	languages	religions	currency
AFGHANISTAN	652 225	251 825	23 294 000	Kābul	Dari, Pushtu, Uzbek, Turkmen	Sunni Muslim, Shi'a Muslim	Afghani
ARMENIA	29 800	11 506	3 790 000	Yerevan	Armenian, Azeri	Armenian Orthodox	Dram
AZERBAIJAN	86 600	33 436	8 147 000	Baku	Azeri, Armenian, Russian, Lezgian	Shi'a Muslim, Sunni Muslim, Russian and Armenian Orthodox	Azerbaijani manat
BAHRAIN	691	267	663 000	Manama	Arabic, English	Shi'a Muslim, Sunni Muslim, Christian	Bahrain dinar
BANGLADESH	143 998	55 598	143 364 000	Dhaka	Bengali, English	Sunni Muslim, Hindu	Taka
BHUTAN	46 620	18 000	2 198 000	Thimphu	Dzongkha, Nepali, Assamese	Buddhist, Hindu	Ngultrum, Indian rupee
BRUNEI	5 765	2 226	341 000	Bandar Seri Begawan	Malay, English, Chinese	Sunni Muslim, Buddhist, Christian	Brunei dollar
CAMBODIA	181 000	69 884	13 776 000	Phnom Penh	Khmer, Vietnamese	Buddhist, Roman Catholic, Sunni Muslim	Riel
CHINA	9 584 492	3 700 593	1 279 557 000	Beijing	Mandarin, Wu, Cantonese, Hsiang, regional languages	Confucian, Taoist, Buddhist, Christian, Sunni Muslim	Yuan, HK dollar*, Macau pataca
CYPRUS	9 251	3 572	797 000	Nicosia	Greek, Turkish, English	Greek Orthodox, Sunni Muslim	Cyprus pound
EAST TIMOR	14 874	5 743	779 000	Dili	Portuguese, Tetun, English	Roman Catholic	United States dollar
GEORGIA	69 700	26 911	5 213 000	T'bilisi	Georgian, Russian, Armenian, Azeri, Ossetian, Abkhaz	Georgian Orthodox, Russian Orthodox, Sunni Muslim	Lari
INDIA	3 065 027	1 183 414	1 041 144 000	New Delhi	Hindi, English, many regional languages	Hindu, Sunni Muslim, Shi'a Muslim, Sikh, Christian	Indian rupee
INDONESIA	1 919 445	741 102	217 534 000	Jakarta	Indonesian, local languages	Sunni Muslim, Protestant, Roman Catholic, Hindu, Buddhist	Rupiah
IRAN	1 648 000	636 296	72 376 000	Tehrān	Farsi, Azeri, Kurdish, regional languages	Shi'a Muslim, Sunni Muslim	Iranian rial
IRAQ	438 317	169 235	24 246 000	Baghdād	Arabic, Kurdish, Turkmen	Shi'a Muslim, Sunni Muslim, Christian	Iraqi dinar
ISRAEL	20 770	8 019	6 303 000	Jerusalem	Hebrew, Arabic	Jewish, Sunni Muslim, Christian, Druze	Shekel
JAPAN	377 727	145 841	127 538 000	Tōkyō	Japanese	Shintoist, Buddhist, Christian	Yen
JORDAN	89 206	34 443	5 196 000	'Ammān	Arabic	Sunni Muslim, Christian	Jordanian dinar
KAZAKHSTAN	2 717 300	1 049 155	16 027 000	Astana	Kazakh, Russian, Ukrainian, German, Uzbek, Tatar	Sunni Muslim, Russian Orthodox, Protestant	Tenge
KUWAIT	17 818	6 880	2 023 000	Kuwait	Arabic	Sunni Muslim, Shi'a Muslim, Christian, Hindu	Kuwaiti dinar
KYRGYZSTAN	198 500	76 641	5 047 000	Bishkek	Kyrgyz, Russian, Uzbek	Sunni Muslim, Russian Orthodox	Kyrgyz som
LAOS	236 800	91 429	5 530 000	Vientiane	Lao, local languages	Buddhist, traditional beliefs	Kip
LEBANON	10 452	4 036	3 614 000	Beirut	Arabic, Armenian, French	Shi'a Muslim, Sunni Muslim, Christian	Lebanese pound
MALAYSIA	332 965	128 559	23 036 000	Kuala Lumpur/Putrajaya	Malay, English, Chinese, Tamil, local languages	Sunni Muslim, Buddhist, Hindu, Christian, traditional beliefs	Ringgit
MALDIVES	298	115	309 000	Male	Divehi (Maldivian)	Sunni Muslim	Rufiyaa

*Hong Kong dollar

ASIA continued

ASIA continued	area sq km	area sq miles	population	capital	languages	religions	currency
MONGOLIA	1 565 000	604 250	2 587 000	Ulan Bator	Khalka (Mongolian), Kazakh, local languages	Buddhist, Sunni Muslim	Tugrik (tögrög)
MYANMAR	676 577	261 228	48 956 000	Rangoon	Burmese, Shan, Karen, local languages	Buddhist, Christian, Sunni Muslim	Kyat
NEPAL	147 181	56 827	24 153 000	Kathmandu	Nepali, Maithili, Bhojpuri, English, local languages	Hindu, Buddhist, Sunni Muslim	Nepalese rupee
NORTH KOREA	120 538	46 540	22 586 000	P'yŏngyang	Korean	Traditional beliefs, Chondoist, Buddhist	North Korean won
OMAN	309 500	119 499	2 709 000	Muscat	Arabic, Baluchi, Indian languages	Ibadhi Muslim, Sunni Muslim	Omani riyal
PAKISTAN	803 940	310 403	148 721 000	Islamabad	Urdu, Punjabi, Sindhi, Pushtu, English	Sunni Muslim, Shi'a Muslim, Christian, Hindu	Pakistani rupee
PALAU	497	192	20 000	Koror	Palauan, English	Roman Catholic, Protestant, traditional beliefs	United States dollar
PHILIPPINES	300 000	115 831	78 611 000	Manila	English, Pilipino, Cebuano, local languages	Roman Catholic, Protestant, Sunni Muslim, Aglipayan	Philippine peso
QATAR	11 437	4 416	584 000	Doha	Arabic	Sunni Muslim	Qatari riyal
RUSSIAN FEDERATION	17 075 400	6 592 849	143 752 000	Moscow	Russian, Tatar, Ukrainian, local languages	Russian Orthodox, Sunni Muslim, Protestant	Russian rouble
SAUDI ARABIA	2 200 000	849 425	21 701 000	Riyadh	Arabic	Sunni Muslim, Shi'a Muslim	Saudi Arabian riyal
SINGAPORE	639	247	4 188 000	Singapore	Chinese, English, Malay, Tamil	Buddhist, Taoist, Sunni Muslim, Christian, Hindu	Singapore dollar
SOUTH KOREA	99 274	38 330	47 389 000	Seoul	Korean	Buddhist, Protestant, Roman Catholic	South Korean won
SRI LANKA	65 610	25 332	19 287 000	Sri Jayewardenepura Kotte	Sinhalese, Tamil, English	Buddhist, Hindu, Sunni Muslim, Roman Catholic	Sri Lankan rupee
SYRIA	185 180	71 498	17 040 000	Damascus	Arabic, Kurdish, Armenian	Sunni Muslim, Shi'a Muslim, Christian	Syrian pound
TAIWAN	36 179	13 969	22 548 000	T'aipei	Mandarin, Min, Hakka, local languages	Buddhist, Taoist, Confucian, Christian	Taiwan dollar
TAJIKISTAN	143 100	55 251	6 177 000	Dushanbe	Tajik, Uzbek, Russian	Sunni Muslim	Somoni
THAILAND	513 115	198 115	64 344 000	Bangkok	Thai, Lao, Chinese, Malay, Mon–Khmer languages	Buddhist, Sunni Muslim	Baht
TURKEY	779 452	300 948	68 569 000	Ankara	Turkish, Kurdish	Sunni Muslim, Shi'a Muslim	Turkish lira
TURKMENISTAN	488 100	188 456	4 930 000	Ashgabat	Turkmen, Uzbek, Russian	Sunni Muslim, Russian Orthodox	Turkmen manat
UNITED ARAB EMIRATES	83 600	32 278	2 701 000	Abu Dhabi	Arabic, English	Sunni Muslim, Shi'a Muslim	United Arab Emirates dirham
UZBEKISTAN	447 400	172 742	25 618 000	Tashkent	Uzbek, Russian, Tajik, Kazakh	Sunni Muslim, Russian Orthodox	Uzbek som
VIETNAM	329 565	127 246	80 226 000	Ha Nôi	Vietnamese, Thai, Khmer, Chinese, local languages	Buddhist, Taoist, Roman Catholic, Cao Dai, Hoa Hao	Dong
YEMEN	527 968	203 850	19 912 000	Şan'ā'	Arabic	Sunni Muslim, Shi'a Muslim	Yemeni rial

AFRICA

AFRICA	area sq km	area sq miles	population	capital	languages	religions	currency
ALGERIA	2 381 741	919 595	31 403 000	Algiers	Arabic, French, Berber	Sunni Muslim	Algerian dinar
ANGOLA	1 246 700	481 354	13 936 000	Luanda	Portuguese, Bantu, local languages	Roman Catholic, Protestant, traditional beliefs	Kwanza
BENIN	112 620	43 483	6 629 000	Porto-Novo	French, Fon, Yoruba, Adja, local languages	Traditional beliefs, Roman Catholic, Sunni Muslim	CFA franc*
BOTSWANA	581 370	224 468	1 564 000	Gaborone	English, Setswana, Shona, local languages	Traditional beliefs, Protestant, Roman Catholic	Pula
BURKINA	274 200	105 869	12 207 000	Ouagadougou	French, Moore (Mossi), Fulani, local languages	Sunni Muslim, traditional beliefs, Roman Catholic	CFA franc*
BURUNDI	27 835	10 747	6 688 000	Bujumbura	Kirundi (Hutu, Tutsi), French	Roman Catholic, traditional beliefs, Protestant	Burundian franc
CAMEROON	475 442	183 569	15 535 000	Yaoundé	French, English, Fang, Bamileke, local languages	Roman Catholic, traditional beliefs, Sunni Muslim, Protestant	CFA franc*
CAPE VERDE	4 033	1 557	446 000	Praia	Portuguese, creole	Roman Catholic, Protestant	Cape Verde escudo
CENTRAL AFRICAN REPUBLIC	622 436	240 324	3 844 000	Bangui	French, Sango, Banda, Baya, local languages	Protestant, Roman Catholic, traditional beliefs, Sunni Muslim	CFA franc*
CHAD	1 284 000	495 755	8 390 000	Ndjamena	Arabic, French, Sara, local languages	Sunni Muslim, Roman Catholic, Protestant, traditional beliefs	CFA franc*
COMOROS	1 862	719	749 000	Moroni	Comorian, French, Arabic	Sunni Muslim, Roman Catholic	Comoros franc
CONGO	342 000	132 047	3 206 000	Brazzaville	French, Kongo, Monokutuba, local languages	Roman Catholic, Protestant, traditional beliefs, Sunni Muslim	CFA franc*
CONGO, DEMOCRATIC REP. OF	2 345 410	905 568	54 275 000	Kinshasa	French, Lingala, Swahili, Kongo, local languages	Christian, Sunni Muslim	Congolese franc
CÔTE D'IVOIRE	322 463	124 504	16 691 000	Yamoussoukro	French, creole, Akan, local languages	Sunni Muslim, Roman Catholic, traditional beliefs, Protestant	CFA franc*
DJIBOUTI	23 200	8 958	652 000	Djibouti	Somali, Afar, French, Arabic	Sunni Muslim, Christian	Djibouti franc
EGYPT	1 000 250	386 199	70 278 000	Cairo	Arabic	Sunni Muslim, Coptic Christian	Egyptian pound
EQUATORIAL GUINEA	28 051	10 831	483 000	Malabo	Spanish, French, Fang	Roman Catholic, traditional beliefs	CFA franc*
ERITREA	117 400	45 328	3 993 000	Asmara	Tigrinya, Tigre	Sunni Muslim, Coptic Christian	Nakfa
ETHIOPIA	1 133 880	437 794	66 040 000	Addis Ababa	Oromo, Amharic, Tigrinya, local languages	Ethiopian Orthodox, Sunni Muslim, traditional beliefs	Birr
GABON	267 667	103 347	1 293 000	Libreville	French, Fang, local languages	Roman Catholic, Protestant, traditional beliefs	CFA franc*
THE GAMBIA	11 295	4 361	1 371 000	Banjul	English, Malinke, Fulani, Wolof	Sunni Muslim, Protestant	Dalasi
GHANA	238 537	92 100	20 176 000	Accra	English, Hausa, Akan, local languages	Christian, Sunni Muslim, traditional beliefs	Cedi
GUINEA	245 857	94 926	8 381 000	Conakry	French, Fulani, Malinke, local languages	Sunni Muslim, traditional beliefs, Christian	Guinea franc
GUINEA-BISSAU	36 125	13 948	1 257 000	Bissau	Portuguese, crioulo, local languages	Traditional beliefs, Sunni Muslim, Christian	CFA franc*
KENYA	582 646	224 961	31 904 000	Nairobi	Swahili, English, local languages	Christian, traditional beliefs	Kenyan shilling
LESOTHO	30 355	11 720	2 076 000	Maseru	Sesotho, English, Zulu	Christian, traditional beliefs	Loti, S. African rand
LIBERIA	111 369	43 000	3 298 000	Monrovia	English, creole, local languages	Traditional beliefs, Christian, Sunni Muslim	Liberian dollar
LIBYA	1 759 540	679 362	5 529 000	Tripoli	Arabic, Berber	Sunni Muslim	Libyan dinar
MADAGASCAR	587 041	226 658	16 913 000	Antananarivo	Malagasy, French	Traditional beliefs, Christian, Sunni Muslim	Malagasy franc
MALAWI	118 484	45 747	11 828 000	Lilongwe	Chichewa, English, local languages	Christian, traditional beliefs, Sunni Muslim	Malawian kwacha
MALI	1 240 140	478 821	12 019 000	Bamako	French, Bambara, local languages	Sunni Muslim, traditional beliefs, Christian	CFA franc*
MAURITANIA	1 030 700	397 955	2 830 000	Nouakchott	Arabic, French, local languages	Sunni Muslim	Ouguiya
MAURITIUS	2 040	788	1 180 000	Port Louis	English, creole, Hindi, Bhojpurī, French	Hindu, Roman Catholic, Sunni Muslim	Mauritius rupee
MOROCCO	446 550	172 414	30 988 000	Rabat	Arabic, Berber, French	Sunni Muslim	Moroccan dirham
MOZAMBIQUE	799 380	308 642	18 986 000	Maputo	Portuguese, Makua, Tsonga, local languages	Traditional beliefs, Roman Catholic, Sunni Muslim	Metical
NAMIBIA	824 292	318 261	1 819 000	Windhoek	English, Afrikaans, German, Ovambo, local languages	Protestant, Roman Catholic	Namibian dollar
NIGER	1 267 000	489 191	11 641 000	Niamey	French, Hausa, Fulani, local languages	Sunni Muslim, traditional beliefs	CFA franc*
NIGERIA	923 768	356 669	120 047 000	Abuja	English, Hausa, Yoruba, Ibo, Fulani, local languages	Sunni Muslim, Christian, traditional beliefs	Naira
RWANDA	26 338	10 169	8 148 000	Kigali	Kinyarwanda, French, English	Roman Catholic, traditional beliefs, Protestant	Rwandan franc
SÃO TOMÉ AND PRÍNCIPE	964	372	143 000	São Tomé	Portuguese, creole	Roman Catholic, Protestant	Dobra
SENEGAL	196 720	75 954	9 908 000	Dakar	French, Wolof, Fulani, local languages	Sunni Muslim, Roman Catholic, traditional beliefs	CFA franc*
SEYCHELLES	455	176	83 000	Victoria	English, French, creole	Roman Catholic, Protestant	Seychelles rupee

*Communauté Financière Africaine

AFRICA continued	area sq km	area sq miles	population	capital	languages	religions	currency
SIERRA LEONE	71 740	27 699	4 814 000	Freetown	English, creole, Mende, Temne, local languages	Sunni Muslim, traditional beliefs	Leone
SOMALIA	637 657	246 201	9 557 000	Mogadishu	Somali, Arabic	Sunni Muslim	Somali shilling
SOUTH AFRICA, REPUBLIC OF	1 219 090	470 693	44 203 000	Pretoria/Cape Town	Afrikaans, English, nine official local languages	Protestant, Roman Catholic, Sunni Muslim, Hindu	Rand
SUDAN	2 505 813	967 500	32 559 000	Khartoum	Arabic, Dinka, Nubian, Beja, Nuer, local languages	Sunni Muslim, traditional beliefs, Christian	Sudanese dinar
SWAZILAND	17 364	6 704	948 000	Mbabane	Swazi, English	Christian, traditional beliefs	Emalangeni, S. African rand
TANZANIA	945 087	364 900	36 820 000	Dodoma	Swahili, English, Nyamwezi, local languages	Shi'a Muslim, Sunni Muslim, traditional beliefs, Christian	Tanzanian shilling
TOGO	56 785	21 925	4 779 000	Lomé	French, Ewe, Kabre, local languages	Traditional beliefs, Christian, Sunni Muslim	CFA franc*
TUNISIA	164 150	63 379	9 670 000	Tunis	Arabic, French	Sunni Muslim	Tunisian dinar
UGANDA	241 038	93 065	24 780 000	Kampala	English, Swahili, Luganda, local languages	Roman Catholic, Protestant, Sunni Muslim, traditional beliefs	Ugandan shilling
ZAMBIA	752 614	290 586	10 872 000	Lusaka	English, Bemba, Nyanja, Tonga, local languages	Christian, traditional beliefs	Zambian kwacha
ZIMBABWE	390 759	150 873	13 076 000	Harare	English, Shona, Ndebele	Christian, traditional beliefs	Zimbabwean dollar

*Communauté Financière Africaine

OCEANIA	area sq km	area sq miles	population	capital	languages	religions	currency
AUSTRALIA	7 682 395	2 966 189	19 536 000	Canberra	English, Italian, Greek	Protestant, Roman Catholic, Orthodox	Australian dollar
FIJI	18 330	7 077	832 000	Suva	English, Fijian, Hindi	Christian, Hindu, Sunni Muslim	Fiji dollar
KIRIBATI	717	277	85 000	Bairiki	Gilbertese, English	Roman Catholic, Protestant	Australian dollar
MARSHALL ISLANDS	181	70	53 000	Delap-Uliga-Djarrit	English, Marshallese	Protestant, Roman Catholic	United States dollar
MICRONESIA, FEDERATED STATES OF	701	271	129 000	Palikir	English, Chuukese, Pohnpeian, local languages	Roman Catholic, Protestant	United States dollar
NAURU	21	8	13 000	Yaren	Nauruan, English	Protestant, Roman Catholic	Australian dollar
NEW ZEALAND	270 534	104 454	3 837 000	Wellington	English, Maori	Protestant, Roman Catholic	New Zealand dollar
PAPUA NEW GUINEA	462 840	178 704	5 032 000	Port Moresby	English, Tok Pisin (creole), local languages	Protestant, Roman Catholic, traditional beliefs	Kina
SAMOA	2 831	1 093	159 000	Apia	Samoan, English	Protestant, Roman Catholic	Tala
SOLOMON ISLANDS	28 370	10 954	479 000	Honiara	English, creole, local languages	Protestant, Roman Catholic	Solomon Islands dollar
TONGA	748	289	100 000	Nuku'alofa	Tongan, English	Protestant, Roman Catholic	Pa'anga
TUVALU	25	10	10 000	Vaiaku	Tuvaluan, English	Protestant	Australian dollar
VANUATU	12 190	4 707	207 000	Port Vila	English, Bislama (creole), French	Protestant, Roman Catholic, traditional beliefs	Vatu

NORTH AMERICA	area sq km	area sq miles	population	capital	languages	religions	currency
ANTIGUA AND BARBUDA	442	171	65 000	St John's	English, creole	Protestant, Roman Catholic	East Caribbean dollar
THE BAHAMAS	13 939	5 382	312 000	Nassau	English, creole	Protestant, Roman Catholic	Bahamian dollar
BARBADOS	430	166	269 000	Bridgetown	English, creole	Protestant, Roman Catholic	Barbados dollar
BELIZE	22 965	8 867	236 000	Belmopan	English, Spanish, Mayan, creole	Roman Catholic, Protestant	Belize dollar
CANADA	9 970 610	3 849 674	31 268 000	Ottawa	English, French	Roman Catholic, Protestant, Eastern Orthodox, Jewish	Canadian dollar
COSTA RICA	51 100	19 730	4 200 000	San José	Spanish	Roman Catholic, Protestant	Costa Rican colón
CUBA	110 860	42 803	11 273 000	Havana	Spanish	Roman Catholic, Protestant	Cuban peso
DOMINICA	750	290	70 000	Roseau	English, creole	Roman Catholic, Protestant	East Caribbean dollar
DOMINICAN REPUBLIC	48 442	18 704	8 639 000	Santo Domingo	Spanish, creole	Roman Catholic, Protestant	Dominican peso
EL SALVADOR	21 041	8 124	6 520 000	San Salvador	Spanish	Roman Catholic, Protestant	El Salvador colón, United States dollar
GRENADA	378	146	94 000	St George's	English, creole	Roman Catholic, Protestant	East Caribbean dollar
GUATEMALA	108 890	42 043	11 995 000	Guatemala City	Spanish, Mayan languages	Roman Catholic, Protestant	Quetzal, United States dollar
HAITI	27 750	10 714	8 400 000	Port-au-Prince	French, creole	Roman Catholic, Protestant, Voodoo	Gourde
HONDURAS	112 088	43 277	6 732 000	Tegucigalpa	Spanish, Amerindian languages	Roman Catholic, Protestant	Lempira
JAMAICA	10 991	4 244	2 621 000	Kingston	English, creole	Protestant, Roman Catholic	Jamaican dollar
MEXICO	1 972 545	761 604	101 842 000	Mexico City	Spanish, Amerindian languages	Roman Catholic, Protestant	Mexican peso
NICARAGUA	130 000	50 193	5 347 000	Managua	Spanish, Amerindian languages	Roman Catholic, Protestant	Córdoba
PANAMA	77 082	29 762	2 942 000	Panama City	Spanish, English, Amerindian languages	Roman Catholic, Protestant, Sunni Muslim	Balboa
ST KITTS AND NEVIS	261	101	38 000	Basseterre	English, creole	Protestant, Roman Catholic	East Caribbean dollar
ST LUCIA	616	238	151 000	Castries	English, creole	Roman Catholic, Protestant	East Caribbean dollar
ST VINCENT AND THE GRENADINES	389	150	115 000	Kingstown	English, creole	Protestant, Roman Catholic	East Caribbean dollar
TRINIDAD AND TOBAGO	5 130	1 981	1 306 000	Port of Spain	English, creole, Hindi	Roman Catholic, Hindu, Protestant, Sunni Muslim	Trinidad and Tobago dollar
UNITED STATES OF AMERICA	9 809 378	3 787 422	288 530 000	Washington DC	English, Spanish	Protestant, Roman Catholic, Sunni Muslim, Jewish	United States dollar

SOUTH AMERICA	area sq km	area sq miles	population	capital	languages	religions	currency
ARGENTINA	2 766 889	1 068 302	37 944 000	Buenos Aires	Spanish, Italian, Amerindian languages	Roman Catholic, Protestant	Argentinian peso
BOLIVIA	1 098 581	424 164	8 705 000	La Paz/Sucre	Spanish, Quechua, Aymara	Roman Catholic, Protestant, Baha'i	Boliviano
BRAZIL	8 547 379	3 300 161	174 706 000	Brasília	Portuguese	Roman Catholic, Protestant	Real
CHILE	756 945	292 258	15 589 000	Santiago	Spanish, Amerindian languages	Roman Catholic, Protestant	Chilean peso
COLOMBIA	1 141 748	440 831	43 495 000	Bogotá	Spanish, Amerindian languages	Roman Catholic, Protestant	Colombian peso
ECUADOR	272 045	105 037	13 112 000	Quito	Spanish, Quechua, other Amerindian languages	Roman Catholic	US dollar
GUYANA	214 969	83 000	765 000	Georgetown	English, creole, Amerindian languages	Protestant, Hindu, Roman Catholic, Sunni Muslim	Guyana dollar
PARAGUAY	406 752	157 048	5 778 000	Asunción	Spanish, Guaraní	Roman Catholic, Protestant	Guaraní
PERU	1 285 216	496 225	26 523 000	Lima	Spanish, Quechua, Aymara	Roman Catholic, Protestant	Sol
SURINAME	163 820	63 251	421 000	Paramaribo	Dutch, Surinamese, English, Hindi	Hindu, Roman Catholic, Protestant, Sunni Muslim	Suriname guilder
URUGUAY	176 215	68 037	3 385 000	Montevideo	Spanish	Roman Catholic, Protestant, Jewish	Uruguayan peso
VENEZUELA	912 050	352 144	25 093 000	Caracas	Spanish, Amerindian languages	Roman Catholic, Protestant	Bolívar

ABBREVIATION KEY

A.	ANDORRA	HUN.	HUNGARY	S.	SERBIA AND MONTENEGRO
AL.	ALBANIA	ISR.	ISRAEL	ROM.	ROMANIA
ARM.	ARMENIA	JOR.	JORDAN	SL.	SLOVENIA
AUST.	AUSTRIA	L.	LUXEMBOURG	SLA.	SLOVAKIA
AZER.	AZERBAIJAN	LAT.	LATVIA	SUR.	SURINAME
B.	BURUNDI	LEB.	LEBANON	SW.	SWITZERLAND
BEL.	BELGIUM	LITH.	LITHUANIA	TAJIK.	TAJIKISTAN
B.H.	BOSNIA-HERZEGOVINA	M.	MACEDONIA	TURKM.	TURKMENISTAN
BULG.	BULGARIA	MOL.	MOLDOVA	U.A.E.	UNITED ARAB EMIRATES
CR.	CROATIA	NETH.	NETHERLANDS	U.K.	UNITED KINGDOM
CZ.R.	CZECH REPUBLIC	N.Z.	NEW ZEALAND	U.S.A.	UNITED STATES OF AMERICA
EST.	ESTONIA	R.	RWANDA	UZBEK.	UZBEKISTAN
GEOR.	GEORGIA	R.F.	RUSSIAN FEDERATION		

World's largest countries (area)

COUNTRY	AREA	
Russian Federation, Europe/Asia	17 075 400 sq km	6 592 849 sq miles
Canada, North America	9 970 610 sq km	3 849 674 sq miles
United States of America, North America	9 809 378 sq km	3 787 422 sq miles
China, Asia	9 584 492 sq km	3 700 593 sq miles
Brazil, South America	8 547 379 sq km	3 300 161 sq miles
Australia, Oceania	7 682 395 sq km	2 966 189 sq miles
India, Asia	3 065 027 sq km	1 183 414 sq miles
Argentina, South America	2 766 889 sq km	1 068 302 sq miles
Kazakhstan, Asia	2 717 300 sq km	1 049 155 sq miles
Sudan, Africa	2 505 813 sq km	967 500 sq miles

World's largest countries (population)

COUNTRY	POPULATION
China, Asia	1 279 557 000
India, Asia	1 041 144 000
United States of America, North America	288 530 000
Indonesia, Asia	217 534 000
Brazil, South America	174 706 000
Pakistan, Asia	148 721 000
Russian Federation, Europe/Asia	143 752 000
Bangladesh, Asia	143 364 000
Japan, Asia	127 538 000
Nigeria, Africa	120 047 000

World's largest cities

CITY	POPULATION
Tōkyō, Japan	26 444 000
Mexico City, Mexico	18 066 000
São Paulo, Brazil	17 962 000
New York, United States of America	16 732 000
Mumbai, India	16 086 000
Los Angeles, United States of America	13 213 000
Kolkata, India	13 058 000
Shanghai, China	12 887 000
Dhaka, Bangladesh	12 519 000
Delhi, India	12 441 000

World capitals

Largest national capital (population)	Tōkyō, Japan	26 444 000	
Smallest national capital (population)	Vatican City	524	
Most northerly national capital	Reykjavík, Iceland	64° 08'N	
Most southerly national capital	Wellington, New Zealand	41° 18'S	
Highest capital	La Paz, Bolivia	3 630 m	11 909 ft
Joint capital (Netherlands)	Amsterdam/The Hague		
Joint capital (Malaysia)	Kuala Lumpur/Putrajaya		
Joint capital (Bolivia)	La Paz/Sucre		
Joint capital (South Africa)	Pretoria/Cape Town		

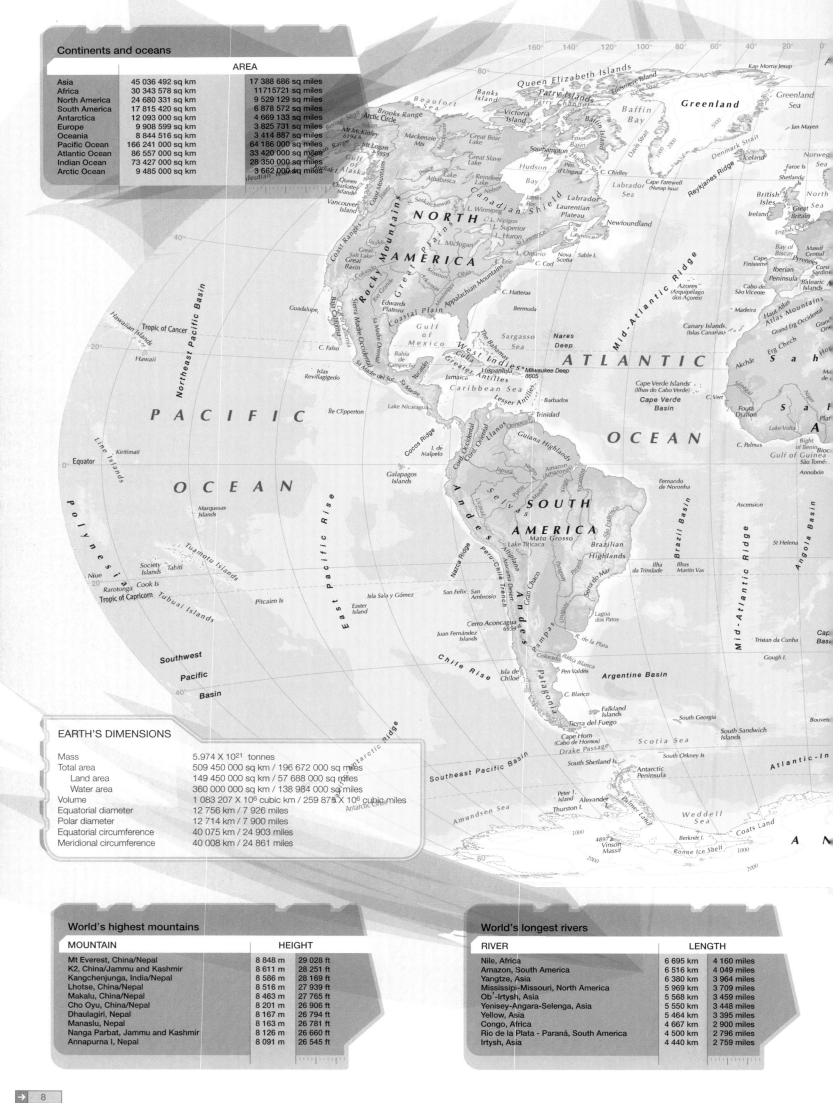

Continents and oceans

	AREA	
Asia	45 036 492 sq km	17 388 686 sq miles
Africa	30 343 578 sq km	11715721 sq miles
North America	24 680 331 sq km	9 529 129 sq miles
South America	17 815 420 sq km	6 878 572 sq miles
Antarctica	12 093 000 sq km	4 669 133 sq miles
Europe	9 908 599 sq km	3 825 731 sq miles
Oceania	8 844 516 sq km	3 414 887 sq miles
Pacific Ocean	166 241 000 sq km	64 186 000 sq miles
Atlantic Ocean	86 557 000 sq km	33 420 000 sq miles
Indian Ocean	73 427 000 sq km	28 350 000 sq miles
Arctic Ocean	9 485 000 sq km	3 662 000 sq miles

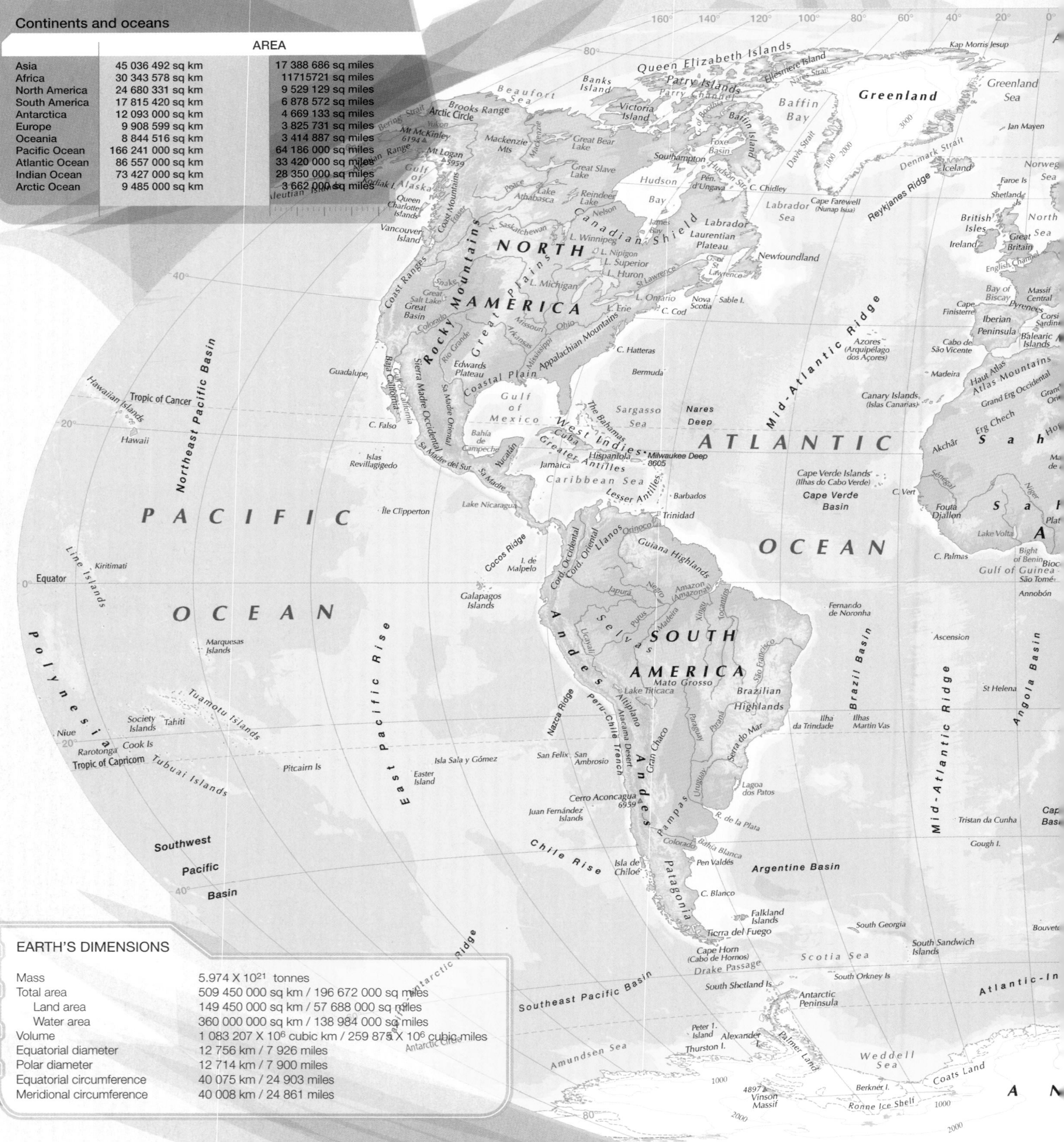

EARTH'S DIMENSIONS

Mass	5.974×10^{21} tonnes
Total area	509 450 000 sq km / 196 672 000 sq miles
Land area	149 450 000 sq km / 57 688 000 sq miles
Water area	360 000 000 sq km / 138 984 000 sq miles
Volume	$1\,083\,207 \times 10^6$ cubic km / $259\,875 \times 10^6$ cubic miles
Equatorial diameter	12 756 km / 7 926 miles
Polar diameter	12 714 km / 7 900 miles
Equatorial circumference	40 075 km / 24 903 miles
Meridional circumference	40 008 km / 24 861 miles

World's highest mountains

MOUNTAIN	HEIGHT	
Mt Everest, China/Nepal	8 848 m	29 028 ft
K2, China/Jammu and Kashmir	8 611 m	28 251 ft
Kangchenjunga, India/Nepal	8 586 m	28 169 ft
Lhotse, China/Nepal	8 516 m	27 939 ft
Makalu, China/Nepal	8 463 m	27 765 ft
Cho Oyu, China/Nepal	8 201 m	26 906 ft
Dhaulagiri, Nepal	8 167 m	26 794 ft
Manaslu, Nepal	8 163 m	26 781 ft
Nanga Parbat, Jammu and Kashmir	8 126 m	26 660 ft
Annapurna I, Nepal	8 091 m	26 545 ft

World's longest rivers

RIVER	LENGTH	
Nile, Africa	6 695 km	4 160 miles
Amazon, South America	6 516 km	4 049 miles
Yangtze, Asia	6 380 km	3 964 miles
Mississipi-Missouri, North America	5 969 km	3 709 miles
Ob'-Irtysh, Asia	5 568 km	3 459 miles
Yenisey-Angara-Selenga, Asia	5 550 km	3 448 miles
Yellow, Asia	5 464 km	3 395 miles
Congo, Africa	4 667 km	2 900 miles
Rio de la Plata - Paraná, South America	4 500 km	2 796 miles
Irtysh, Asia	4 440 km	2 759 miles

World's largest lakes

LAKE	AREA	
Caspian Sea, Asia/Europe	371 000 sq km	143 243 sq miles
Lake Superior, North America	82 100 sq km	31 698 sq miles
Lake Victoria, Africa	68 800 sq km	26 563 sq miles
Lake Huron, North America	59 600 sq km	23 011 sq miles
Lake Michigan, North America	57 800 sq km	22 316 sq miles
Aral Sea, Asia	33 640 sq km	12 988 sq miles
Lake Tanganyika, Africa	32 900 sq km	12 702 sq miles
Great Bear Lake, North America	31 328 sq km	12 095 sq miles
Lake Baikal, Asia	30 500 sq km	11 776 sq miles
Lake Nyasa, Africa	30 044 sq km	11 600 sq miles

World's largest islands

ISLAND	AREA	
Greenland, North America	2 175 600 sq km	840 004 sq miles
New Guinea, Oceania	808 510 sq km	312 167 sq miles
Borneo, Asia	745 561 sq km	287 863 sq miles
Madagascar, Africa	587 040 sq km	266 657 sq miles
Baffin Island, North America	507 451 sq km	195 927 sq miles
Sumatra, Asia	473 606 sq km	182 860 sq miles
Honshū, Asia	227 414 sq km	87 805 sq miles
Great Britain, Europe	218 476 sq km	84 354 sq miles
Victoria Island, North America	217 291 sq km	83 897 sq miles
Ellesmere Island, North America	196 236 sq km	75 767 sq miles

Conic Equidistant Projection

10

1:5 000 000

0 50 100 150 miles

0 50 100 150 200 250 km

NORWAY
OSLO
DENMARK
COPENHAGEN (København)
GERMANY
BERLIN
POLAND
WARSAW (Warszawa)
LITHUANIA
VILNIUS
LATVIA
RIGA
ESTONIA
TALLINN
BELARUS
MINSK
RUSSIAN FEDERATION
STOCKHOLM
HELSINKI (Helsingfors)
St Petersburg (Sankt-Peterburg)
LENINGRADSKAYA OBLAST'
PSKOVSKAYA OBLAST'
Gulf of Finland
Gulf of Riga
Gulf of Gdańsk
Baltic Sea
Skagerrak
Kattegat
Gotland (Sweden)
Öland
Saaremaa
Hiiumaa
Åland Islands
Bornholm (Denmark)
Zealand
Jutland
Rügen
Lake Peipus
Vänern
Vättern
North Frisian Islands
East Frisian Islands

Conic Equidistant Projection

→ 12

1:5 000 000

0 50 100 150 miles

0 50 100 150 200 250 km

NORWAY
SWEDEN
ESTONIA
LATVIA
LITHUANIA
RUSSIAN FEDERATION
DENMARK
POLAND
GERMANY
CZECH REPUBLIC
SLOVAKIA
AUSTRIA
HUNGARY
SWITZERLAND
LIECHTENSTEIN
ITALY
SLOVENIA
CROATIA
LANDS
Skagerrak
Kattegat
Baltic Sea
Gulf of Riga
Gulf of Gdańsk
Jutland
Zealand
Fyn
Lolland
Falster
Møn
Bornholm (Denmark)
Gotland (Sweden)
Öland
Saaremaa
North Frisian Islands
East Frisian Islands
Helgoland
COPENHAGEN (København)
BERLIN
WARSAW (Warszawa)
PRAGUE (Praha)
VIENNA (Wien)
BRATISLAVA
BUDAPEST
LUXEMBOURG
BERN
VADUZ
Hamburg
Hannover
Bremen
Frankfurt am Main
Munich (München)
Stuttgart
Nuremberg (Nürnberg)
Leipzig
Dresden
Cologne (Köln)
Düsseldorf
Essen
Dortmund
Gothenburg (Göteborg)
Malmö
Gdańsk
Poznań
Wrocław
Kraków
Łódź
Szczecin
Salzburg
Graz
Linz
Innsbruck
Zürich
Basel
BAVARIA
BOHEMIA
MORAVIA
Harz
Vosges
Black Forest
Schwäbische Alb
Erzgebirge
Sudety
Böhmer Wald
Hohe Tauern

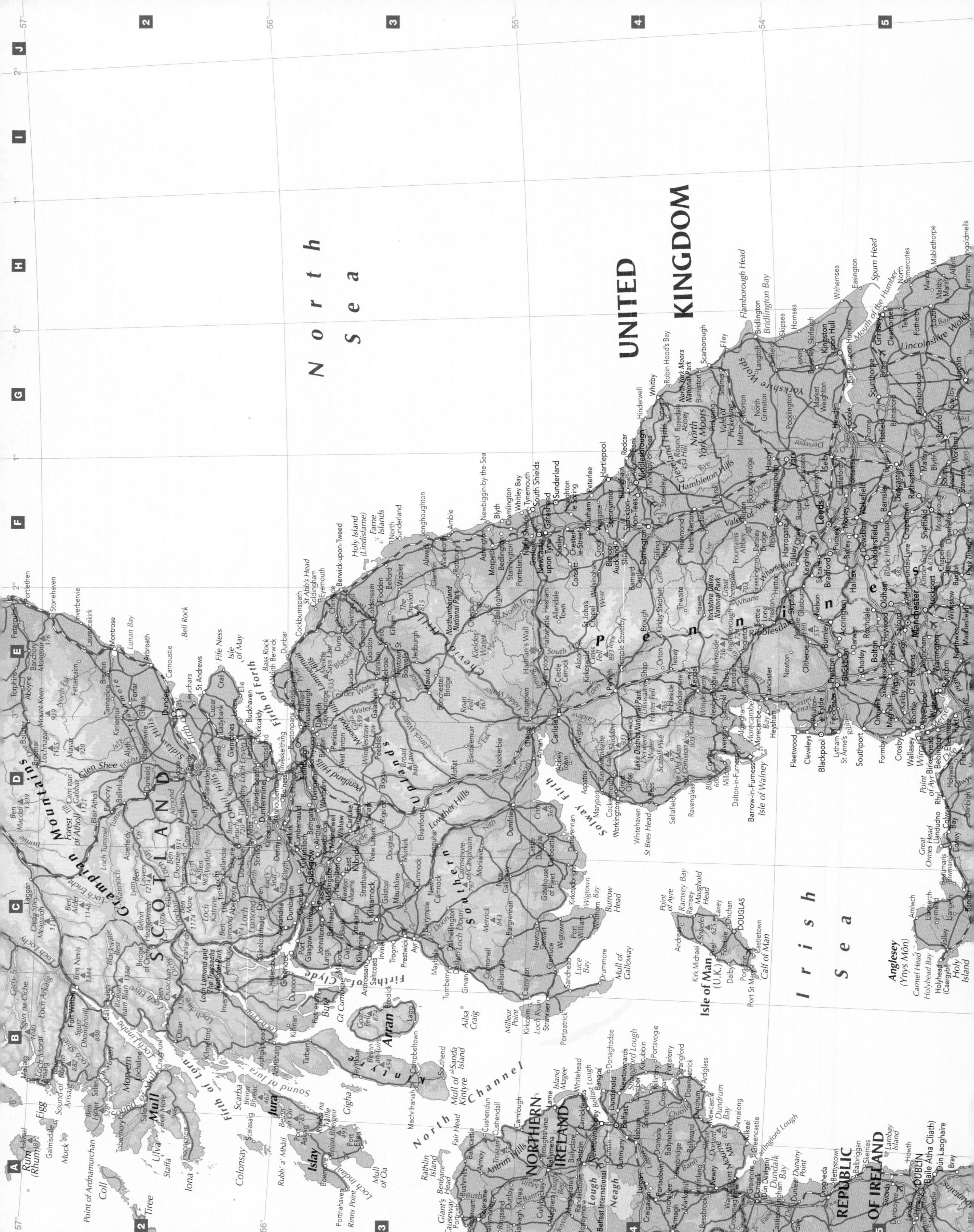

Conic Equidistant Projection

→ 14

1:2 000 000

0 25 50 75 miles

0 25 50 75 100 125 km

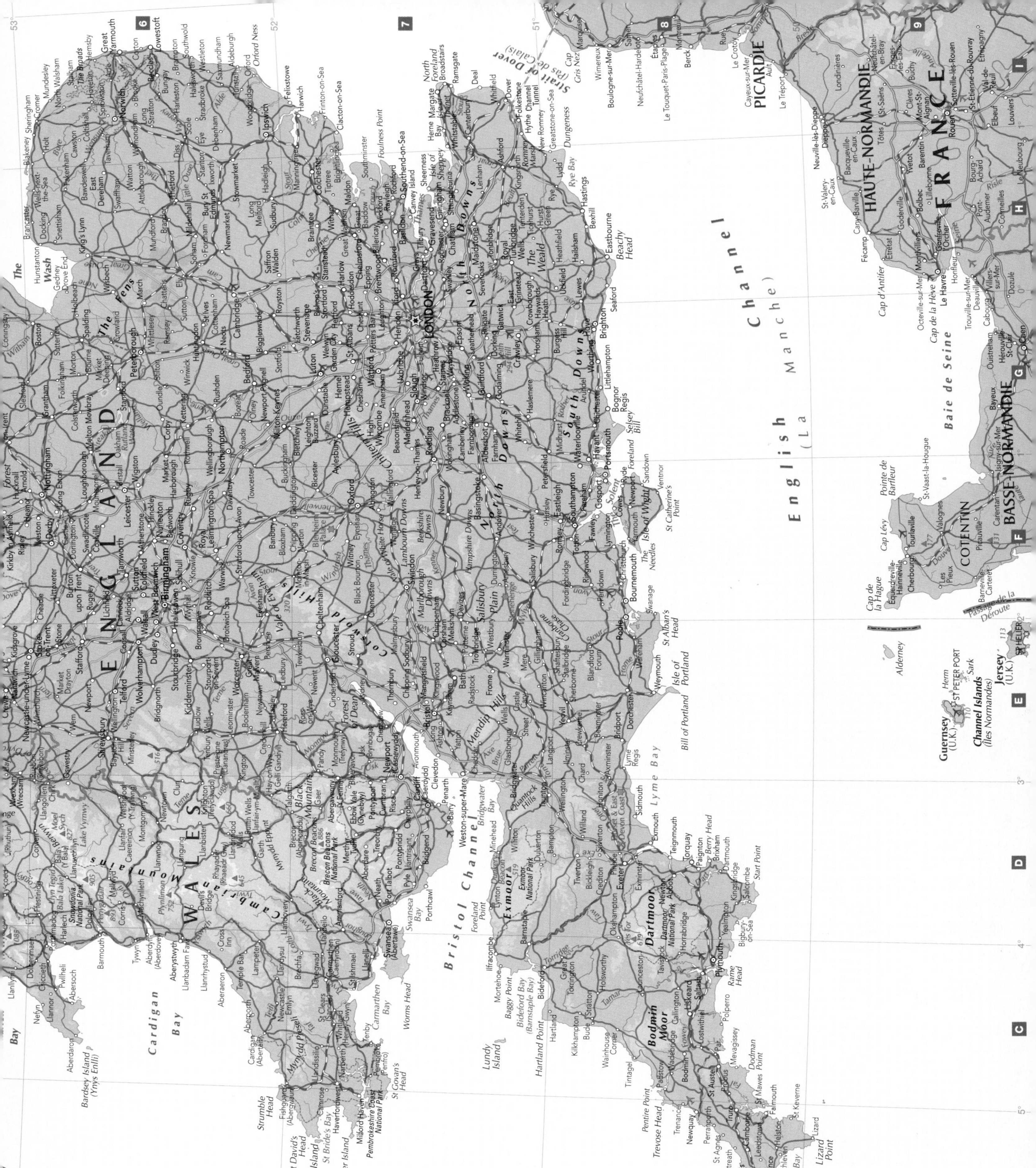
ENGLAND
WALES
FRANCE
LONDON
English Channel
(La Manche)
Bristol Channel
Cardigan Bay
St George's Channel
Strait of Dover
(Pas de Calais)
PICARDIE
HAUTE-NORMANDIE
BASSE-NORMANDIE
COTENTIN
Channel Islands
(îles Normandes)
Isles of Scilly
Baie de Seine
Lyme Bay
The Wash
Cambrian Mountains
North Downs
South Downs
Dartmoor
Exmoor
Bodmin Moor
Salisbury Plain
Cotswolds
Chiltern Hills
The Fens
The Broads
Birmingham
Bristol
Cardiff
Southampton
Portsmouth
Plymouth
Norwich
Brighton
Oxford
Cambridge
Swansea
Guernsey
Jersey
Alderney
Land's End
Lizard Point

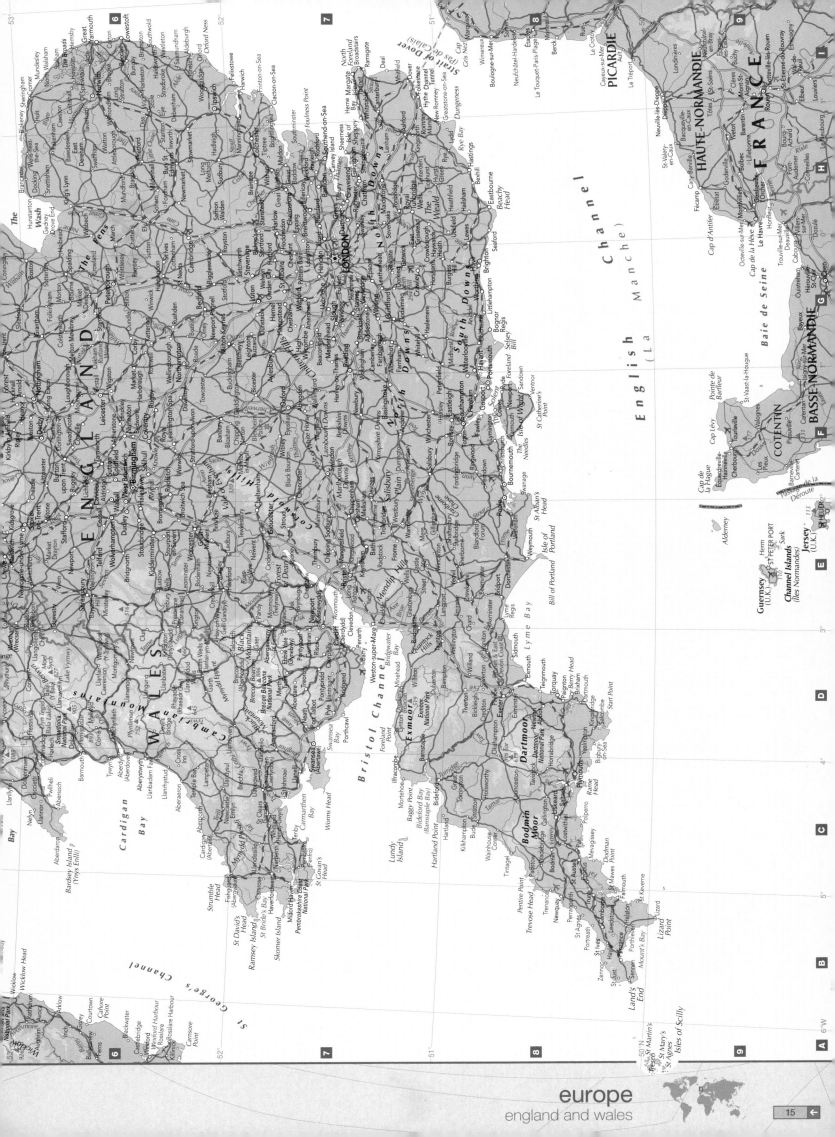

europe
scotland

1:2 000 000
0 25 50 75 miles
0 25 50 75 100 125 km

Conic Equidistant Projection

1:2 000 000
0 25 50 75 miles
0 25 50 75 100 125 km

Conic Equidistant Projection

europe

france

1:5 000 000

0 50 100 150 miles

0 50 100 150 200 250 km

Conic Equidistant Projection

1:5 000 000

0 50 100 150 miles

0 50 100 150 200 250 km

Conic Equidistant Projection

→ 20

1:5 000 000

0 50 100 150 miles

0 50 100 150 200 250 km

UKRAINE
MOLDOVA
CHIȘINĂU (Kishinev)
ROMANIA
BUCHAREST (București)
Transylvanian Alps
Carpathian Mountains
Transylvanian Basin (Podișul Transilvaniei)
DOBRUJA
SERBIA AND MONTENEGRO
SRBIJA (SERBIA)
BELGRADE (Beograd)
VOJVODINA
KOSOVO
BULGARIA
SOFIA (Sofiya)
Balkan Mountains
Stara Planina
Sredna Gora
Rhodope Mountains
THRACE
LUDOGORIE
MACEDONIA
SKOPJE
ALBANIA
TIRANA (Tiranë)
GREECE
ATHENS (Athina)
Thessaloniki
Peloponnese
Pindus Mountains
Evvoia
Cyclades (Kyklades)
Dodecanese (Dodekanisos)
Crete (Kriti)
Rhodes (Rodos)
Lesbos (Lesvos)
Chios
Samos
Corfu (Kerkyra)
Cephalonia (Kefallonia)
Zakynthos (Zante)
Aegean Sea
Mirtoö Pelagos
Krytiko Pelagos
Ionian Islands
Sea
Black Sea
Sea of Marmara (Marmara Denizi)
TURKEY
İstanbul
İzmir (Smyrna)
Bursa
Antalya
Crimea (Krymskyy Pivostriv)
Odesa
Danube

Conic Equidistant Projection

→ 22

1:7 500 000

0 100 200 300 miles

0 100 200 300 400 500 km

FEDERATION
BELARUS
UKRAINE
POLAND
SLOVAKIA
HUNGARY
ROMANIA
MOLDOVA
BULGARIA
GREECE
TURKEY
GEORGIA
ARMENIA
AZER.
KAZAKHSTAN
Black Sea
Sea of Azov
Caspian Sea
Crimea

Conic Equidistant Projection

→ 24

1:20 000 000

0 200 400 600 miles
0 200 400 600 800 1000 km

OCEAN
Severnaya Zemlya
New Siberia Islands (Novosibirskiye Ostrova)
East Siberian Sea (Vostochno-Sibirskoye More)
Laptev Sea (More Laptevykh)
Chukchi Sea
Wrangel Island (Ostrov Vrangelya)
Bering Strait
Seward Peninsula
U.S.A.
Norton Sound
St Lawrence Island
Bering Sea
Aleutian Islands
Arctic Circle
Chukotskiy Poluostrov
Koryakskiy Khrebet
Khrebet Kolymskiy
Kolymskaya Nizmennost'
Yukagirskoye Ploskogor'ye
Khrebet Cherskogo
Verkhoyanskiy Khrebet
Central Siberian Plateau
Sredne-Sibirskoye Ploskogor'ye
SIBERIA (SIBIR')
RUSSIAN FEDERATION
Sea of Okhotsk (Okhotskoye More)
Kamchatka Peninsula (Poluostrov Kamchatka)
Petropavlovsk-Kamchatskiy
Magadan
Yakutsk
Khrebet Dzhugdzhur
Stanovoy Khrebet
Stanovoye Nagor'ye
Sakhalin
Yuzhno-Sakhalinsk
Kuril Islands (Kuril'skiye Ostrova)
ADMINISTERED BY RUSSIAN FEDERATION, CLAIMED BY JAPAN
La Pérouse Strait
Khabarovsk
Sikhote-Alin
Vladivostok
Irkutsk
Lake Baikal (Ozero Baykal)
Ulan-Ude
Chita
Harbin
ULAN BATOR (Ulaanbaatar)
MONGOLIA
Gobi
CHINA
BEIJING (Peking)
Tianjin
Shenyang
Da Hinggan Ling
Xiao Hinggan Ling
Bo Hai
Yellow Sea (Huang Hai)
NORTH KOREA
P'YONGYANG
SOUTH KOREA
SEOUL (Soul)
Pusan
Sea of Japan (East Sea)
JAPAN
Hokkaido
Sapporo
Honshu
TOKYO
Yokohama
Nagoya
Osaka
Kyoto
Kobe
Hiroshima
Shikoku
Kyushu
Fukuoka
PACIFIC OCEAN

Albers Conic Equal Area Projection

→ 26

1:20 000 000

Scale: 0 – 200 – 400 – 600 miles; 0 – 200 – 400 – 600 – 800 – 1000 km

RUSSIAN FEDERATION
MONGOLIA
CHINA
KYRGYZSTAN
NEPAL
BHUTAN
BANGLADESH
INDIA
MYANMAR
THAILAND
LAOS
VIETNAM
CAMBODIA
MALAYSIA
INDONESIA
SINGAPORE
SRI LANKA
MALDIVES
Gobi
Altai Mountains
Tien Shan
Tarim Basin
(Tarim Pendi)
Taklimakan Desert
(Taklimakan Shamo)
Kunlun Shan
Altun Shan
Plateau of Tibet
(Qingzang Gaoyuan)
Himalaya
Qaidam Pendi
Qilian Shan
Bay of Bengal
Andaman Sea
Gulf of Thailand
South China Sea
Gulf of Tongking
Bo Hai
Strait of Malacca
Arabian Sea
Deccan
Western Ghats
Eastern Ghats
Malabar Coast
Coromandel Coast
Andaman Islands
(India)
Nicobar Islands
(India)
Lakshadweep
ULAN BATOR
(Ulaanbaatar)
BEIJING
(Peking)
NEW DELHI
KATHMANDU
THIMPHU
DHAKA
(Dacca)
RANGOON
(Yangon)
BANGKOK
(Krung Thep)
VIENTIANE
(Viangchan)
HA NOI
PHNOM PENH
KUALA LUMPUR
SRI JAYEWARDENEPURA KOTTE
BISHKEK
ISLAMABAD
ASTANA
(Akmola)
Mumbai
(Bombay)
Kolkata
(Calcutta)
Chennai
(Madras)
Hong Kong
Ho Chi Minh City
(Saigon)
AKSAI CHIN
CLAIMED BY INDIA,
UNDER CHINESE
ADMIN.
JAMMU AND
KASHMIR
Tropic of Cancer
Equator
G
H
I
J
K
L
2
3
4
5
6

1:20 000 000 — 0 200 400 600 miles; 0 200 400 600 800 1000 km

PACIFIC OCEAN
INDIAN OCEAN
PHILIPPINES
MALAYSIA
INDONESIA
AUSTRALIA
THAILAND
CAMBODIA
VIETNAM
LAOS
BRUNEI
SINGAPORE
EAST TIMOR
PAPUA NEW GUINEA
PALAU
FEDERATED STATES OF MICRONESIA
Northern Mariana Islands (U.S.A.)
Guam (U.S.A.)
South China Sea
Philippine Sea
Sulu Sea
Celebes Sea
Banda Sea
Arafura Sea
Timor Sea
Java Sea
Andaman Sea
Gulf of Thailand
Gulf of Carpentaria
Strait of Malacca
Borneo
Sumatra (Sumatera)
Java (Jawa)
Celebes (Sulawesi)
Moluccas (Maluku)
New Guinea
Mindanao
Luzon
Palawan
MANILA
BANGKOK
PHNOM PENH
KUALA LUMPUR
JAKARTA
BANDAR SERI BEGAWAN
DILI
KOROR
RANGOON (Yangon)
VIENTIANE
NORTHERN TERRITORY
WESTERN AUSTRALIA
QUEENSLAND
Great Sandy Desert
Tanami Desert
Equator
Tropic of Capricorn
Christmas Island (Australia)
Cocos Islands (Australia)
Ashmore and Cartier Islands (Australia)

Conic Equidistant Projection

1:7 000 000

0 100 200 miles
0 100 200 300 400 km

Sea of Japan
(East Sea)
JAPAN
PACIFIC OCEAN
East China Sea
(Dong Hai)
Yellow Sea
(Huang Hai)
Korea Bay
NORTH KOREA
SOUTH KOREA
P'YŎNGYANG
SEOUL (Sŏul)
TŌKYŌ
Ōsaka
Kyōto
Kōbe
Nagoya
Yokohama
Kawasaki
Sendai
Hiroshima
Fukuoka
Kita-Kyūshū
Kumamoto
Kagoshima
Pusan
Taegu
Taejŏn
Kwangju
Inch'ŏn
Shikoku
Kyūshū
Honshū
Bonin Islands
(Ogasawara-shotō)
(Japan)
Ryukyu Islands
(Nansei-shotō)
(Japan)
Tokara-rettō
Amami-shotō
Okinawa-shotō
Izu-shotō
Ōsumi-shotō
Korea Strait
Cheju-do
Ullŭng-do
(South Korea)
Liancourt Rocks
Oki-shotō
Sado-shima

Lambert Azimuthal Equal Area Projection

→ 32

1:16 000 000
0 200 400 miles
0 200 400 600 800 km

Mediterranean Sea
ITALY
Sicily
GREECE
TURKEY
CYPRUS
NICOSIA
SYRIA
LEBANON
BEIRUT
DAMASCUS
IRAQ
BAGHDAD
IRAN
ISRAEL
JERUSALEM
JORDAN
'AMMAN
KUWAIT
LIBYA
CYRENAICA
Gulf of Sirte
EGYPT
CAIRO
Alexandria
Libyan Desert
Great Sand Sea
SAUDI ARABIA
RIYADH
Tropic of Cancer
Mecca
Medina
Red Sea
Nubian Desert
SUDAN
KHARTOUM
Omdurman
CHAD
NDJAMENA
Tibesti
ERITREA
ASMARA
YEMEN
ŞAN'Ā'
DJIBOUTI
Gulf of Aden
ETHIOPIA
ADDIS ABABA
SOMALIA
MOGADISHU
OGADEN
CENTRAL AFRICAN REPUBLIC
BANGUI
DEMOCRATIC REPUBLIC OF CONGO
Congo Basin
CONGO
UGANDA
KAMPALA
KENYA
NAIROBI
Lake Victoria
RWANDA
KIGALI
BURUNDI
BUJUMBURA
TANZANIA
INDIAN OCEAN
Equator

1:16 000 000

miles 0 200 400

km 0 200 400 600 800

DEMOCRATIC REPUBLIC OF CONGO
TANZANIA
ANGOLA
ZAMBIA
MALAWI
MOZAMBIQUE
ZIMBABWE
NAMIBIA
BOTSWANA
REPUBLIC OF SOUTH AFRICA
LESOTHO
SWAZILAND
MADAGASCAR
COMOROS
ATLANTIC OCEAN
INDIAN OCEAN
Mozambique Channel
Kalahari Desert
Namib Desert
Tropic of Capricorn
LUANDA
LUSAKA
HARARE
LILONGWE
MAPUTO
WINDHOEK
GABORONE
PRETORIA
MASERU
MBABANE
ANTANANARIVO
DODOMA
MORONI
Dar es Salaam
Johannesburg
Durban
CAPE TOWN
Port Elizabeth
East London
Bulawayo
Beira
Cape of Good Hope

Lambert Azimuthal Equal Area Projection

→ 36

1:5 000 000

0	100	200	300		miles
0	100	200	300	400	500 km

LIMPOPO
MPUMALANGA
GAUTENG
KWAZULU-NATAL
FREE STATE
EASTERN CAPE
LESOTHO
SWAZILAND
MOZAMBIQUE
GAZA
INHAMBANE
MAPUTO
ZIMBABWE
CENTRAL
KGATLENG
PRETORIA
Johannesburg
Soweto
MASERU
MBABANE
GABORONE
Bloemfontein
Durban
Pietermaritzburg
Port Elizabeth
East London
Richards Bay
Port Shepstone
Kruger National Park
Drakensberg
Tropic of Capricorn
INDIAN
OCEAN

Lambert Azimuthal Equal Area Projection

→ 38

1:20 000 000

0 200 400 600 miles

0 200 400 600 800 1000 km

NAURU
YAREN
Banaba (Ocean Island)
Aranuka
K I R I B A T I
Howland Island (U.S.A.)
Baker Island (U.S.A.)
Nonouti
Beru
Nikunau
Tabiteuea
Onotoa
Kingsmill Group
Tamana
Arorae
Phoenix Islands
Kanton
McKean
Rawaki
Nikumaroro
Orona
Manra
Nukumanu Islands
Tauu Islands
Ontong Java Atoll
SOLOMON ISLANDS
Choiseul
Roncador Reef
Santa Isabel
New Georgia Sound
Buala
New Georgia
Malu'u
Stewart Islands
Florida Islands
Malaita
Maramasike
Ulawa Island
Guadalcanal
Auvavu
Kirakira
Santa Ana
San Cristobal (Makira)
Rennell
Indispensable Reefs
Duff Islands
Nupani
Swallow Islands
Ndeni
Santa Cruz Islands (Solomon Islands)
Utupua
Vanikoro Islands
Mitre Island
Cherry Island
Tikopia
Torres Islands
Uréparapara
Banks Islands
Vanua Lava
Santa María Island
Espíritu Santo
Mount Tabwémasana 1879
Aoba
Maéwo
Pentecost Island
VANUATU
Norsup
Ambrym
Malakula
Epi
Émaé
Shepherd Islands
PORT VILA
Éfaté
Récifs d'Entrecasteaux
Îles Chesterfield (France)
Grand Passage
Erromango
Îles Belep
Grand Récif de Cook
Tanna 361
Futuna
Récif des Français
Nouvelle Calédonie
Anatom (Aneityum)
Koumac
Ouvéa
Îles Loyauté (France)
Lifou
New Caledonia (France)
Tadin
Maré
Bourail
Yaté
NOUMÉA
Île des Pins
Grand Récif du Sud
Nanumea
Nanumanga
Niutao
Nui
Vaitupu
Nukufetau
TUVALU
Funafuti
VAIAKU
Nukulaelae
Niulakita
Tokelau (New Zealand)
Atafu
Nukunono
Fakaofo
Swains Island
Pukapuka (Danger Islands)
Nassau
Rotuma (Fiji)
Wallis and Futuna Islands (France)
Îles Wallis
MATĀ'UTU
SAMOA
Îles de Hoorn
Savai'i
Upolu
APIA
Manua Islands
American Samoa (U.S.A.)
Tutuila
FAGATOGO
Rose Island
Suwarrow
Niuafo'ou 210
Tafahi
Niuatoputapu
Great Sea Reef
Vanua Levu
Yasawa Group
Bligh Water
Labasa (Lambasa)
Lautoka
Tomanivi (Mt. Victoria)
Taveuni
Koro
Viti Levu
Northern Lau Group
SUVA
Koro Sea
Gau
FIJI
Kadavu Passage
Lakeba
Moala
Kadavu
Matuku
Southern Lau Group
Kabara
Vava'u Group
Vatoa
Tofua 500
Cook Islands (New Zealand)
ALOFI
Niue (New Zealand)
Palmerston
Ha'apai Group
Doi
Ono-i-Lau
Ceva-i-Ra (Conway Reef)
Hunter Island 100
TONGA
NUKU'ALOFA
Tongatapu Group
Ata
Minerva Reefs
Tropic of Capricorn
P A C I F I C O C E A N
Norfolk Island (Australia)
KINGSTON
Lord Howe Island (Australia)
Raoul Island
Kermadec Islands (New Zealand)
Macauley Island
Curtis Island
Havre Rock
L'Espérance Rock
Three Kings Islands
North Cape
Cape Maria van Diemen
Awanui
Whangarei
North Island
Great Barrier Island
Takapuna
Auckland
Manukau
NEW ZEALAND
Tasman Sea
Hamilton
Tauranga
East Cape
Tokoroa
Te Kuiti
Whakatane
New Plymouth
Taupo
Gisborne
Mount Taranaki (Mount Egmont)
Wairoa
Mount Ruapehu
Mahia Peninsula
Hawera
Wanganui
Napier
Hastings
Cape Farewell
Palmerston North
Tasman Bay
Levin
South Island
Westport
Nelson
Picton
Masterton
Blenheim
Lower Hutt
Cook Strait
WELLINGTON
Hokitika
Greymouth
Aoraki (Mount Cook) 3754
Southern Alps
Christchurch
Mount Aspiring 3036
Ashburton
Banks Peninsula
Mount Chrisina 2502
Timaru
Queenstown
Oamaru
Cape Providence
Gore
Dunedin
Foveaux Strait
Invercargill
Stewart Island
South West Cape
Snares Islands
Chatham Islands (New Zealand)
Chatham Island
Waitangi
Pitt Island
Bounty Islands (New Zealand)
Antipodes Islands (New Zealand)
Auckland Islands (New Zealand)

INDONESIA
Lombok
Sumbawa
Sumba
Timor
Rote
Savu
Raijua
Kupang
Laut Sawu (Savu Sea)
Timor Sea
Ashmore Reef
Ashmore and Cartier Islands (Australia)
Cartier Island
Browse Island
INDIAN OCEAN
Bonaparte Archipelago
Admiralty Gulf
Kalumburu
Drysdale River National Park
Cape Londonderry
Joseph Bonaparte Gulf
Port Warrender
Brunswick Bay
Champagny Islands
Buccaneer Archipelago
Collier Bay
Cape Lévêque
King Sound
Beagle Bay
DAMPIER LAND
Derby
Kimberley Plateau
King Leopold Ranges
Mount Hann 776
Gibb River
Wyndham
Kununurra
Lake Argyle
Bluff Face Range
Purnululu National Park
Mount Lush 786
Halls Creek
Fitzroy Crossing
Mueller Range
Gantheaume Point
Broome
Roebuck Bay
Lagrange Bay
Cape Bossut
Lagrange
Edgar Ranges
Noonkanbah
McClintock Range
Bohemia Downs
Gordon Downs
Billiluna
Lake Gregory
Balgo
Lewis Range
Eighty Mile Beach
Anna Plains
Larrey Point
Wallal Downs
Great Sandy Desert
South Esk Tableland
Stansmore Range
Lake White
Lake Tobin
Lake Wills
Lake Mackay
Percival Lakes
Lake Waukarlycarly
Dampier Archipelago
Montebello Islands
Barrow Island
Dampier
Karratha
Point Samson
Roebourne
Port Hedland
Goldsworthy
Shay Gap
Marble Bar
Millstream-Chichester National Park
Chichester Range
Abydos
Pannawonica
Hamersley Range
Tom Price
Mount Meharry 1250
Karijini Nat. Park
Newman
Roy Hill
Balfour Downs
Robertson Range
Lake Disappointment
Rudall River National Park
King Hill
Lake Auld
McKay Range
Gibson Desert
Lake Macdonald
Lake Hopkins
Lake Neale
WESTERN AUSTRALIA
AUSTRALIA
North West Cape
Exmouth
Learmonth
Exmouth Gulf
Onslow
Minderoo
Cape Range National Park
Nanutarra Roadhouse
Paraburdoo
Ashburton
Kenneth Range
Coral Bay
Winning
Mundiwindi
Mount Madley 533
Hutton Range
Lake MacLeod
Minilya
Kennedy Range National Park
Mount Augustus 1106
Walburg Range
Collier Range National Park
Mount Essendon 910
Carnarvon Range
Brassey Range
Lake Burnside
Tropic of Capricorn
Geographe Channel
Gascoyne
Bernier Island
Dorre Island
Naturaliste Channel
Cape Inscription
Dirk Hartog Island
Shark Bay
Grey's Plains
Macadam Plains
Robinson Range 802
Milgun
Lake King
Earaheedy
Carnegie
Lake Carnegie
Sutherland Range
Barrow Range
Warburton
Callyharra Springs
Overlander Roadhouse
Beringarra
Meekatharra
Nannine
Lake Annean
Lake Way
Van Truer Tableland
Lake Wells
Ernest Giles Range
Lake Throssell
Francois Peron National Park
Denham
Tamala
Meadow
Errabiddy Hills
Nicholson Range
Cue
Lake Austin
Barr Smith Range
Sandstone
Leinster
Melrose
Mount Shenton 594
Yeo Lake
Great Victoria Desert
Kalbarri National Park
Kalbarri
Murchison
Billabalong
Yuin
Yalgoo
Mount Magnet
Bailey Range
Laverton
Rason Lake
Jubilee Lake
Northampton
Greenough
Mullewa
Thundelarra
Leonora
Malcolm
Lake Carey
Lake Minigwal
Plumridge Lakes
Houtman Abrolhos
Geelvink Channel
Geraldton
Morawa
Mount Singleton
Payne's Find
Lake Barlee
Kookynie
Lake Raeside
Menzies
Edjudina
Lake Ballard
Marmion
Lake Rebecca
Pinjin
Johnston Range
Dongara
Carnamah
Lake Moore
Eneabba
Coorow
Wubin
Beacon
Bonnie Rock
Lake Yindarlgooda
Kalgoorlie
Nullarbor Plain
Loongana
Forrest
Deakin
Rawlinna
Jurien
Cervantes
Moora
Koorda
Mukinbudin
Southern Cross
Coolgardie
Kambalda
Lake Lefroy
Fraser Range
Yellowdine
Bullfinch
Trayning
Gingin
Yanchep
Perth
Fremantle
Rockingham
Mandurah
Pinjarra
Harvey
Bunbury
Northam
York
Merredin
Bruce Rock
Narembeen
Hyden
Lake Johnston
Lake Cowan
Norseman
Lake Dundas
Balladonia
Cocklebiddy
Hampton Tableland
Mundrabilla
Eucla
Corrigin
Pingelly
Kulin
Narrogin
Wickepin
Lake Hope
Frank Hann Nat. Park
Lake Sharpe
Peak Charles 658
Newdegate
Ravensthorpe
Scaddan
Esperance
Cape Arid National Park
Point Culver
Point Malcolm
Cape Arid
Great Australian Bight
Archipelago of the Recherche
Wagin
Katanning
Bluff Knoll 1110
Geographe Bay
Cape Naturaliste
Busselton
Margaret River
Bridgetown
Augusta
Cape Leeuwin
D'Entrecasteaux Nat. Park
Point D'Entrecasteaux
Shannon National Park
Stirling Range National Park
Fitzgerald River National Park
Hood Point
Albany
Denmark
Bald Head
SOUTHERN OCEAN
Cape Van Diemen
Bathurst Island
Melville Island
Croker Island
Cobourg Peninsula
Goulburn Islands
Van Diemen Gulf
Mitchell Point
Beagle Gulf
Charles Point
Darwin
Point Blaze
Anson Bay
Cape Scott
Kakadu National Park
Jabiru
Oenpelli
Maningrida
Batchelor
Adelaide River
Hayes Creek
Pine Creek
El Sharana
Daly River
Wadeye
Dorisvale
Fitzmaurice
Nitmiluk National Park
Katherine
Beswick
Mataranka
Moray Range
Legune
Timber Creek
Victoria River
Gregory National Park
Victoria River Downs
Top Springs
Daly Waters
Dunmarra
Larrimah
Limbunya
Kalkaringi
Lajamanu
Inverway
Nicholson
Birrindudu
Antrim Plateau
NORTHERN TERRITORY
Tanami Desert
Tanami
Rabbit Flat
Lander
Tennant Creek
Willowra
Barrow Creek
Yuendumu
Mount Liebig 1524
Mount Zeil
West MacDonnell Nat. Park
Alice Springs
Macdonnell Ranges
Truer Range
Ehrenberg Range
Watarrka Nat. Park
Finke Gorge Nat. Park
Lake Amadeus
Uluru (Ayers Rock)
Kata Tjuta Nat. Park
Mount Ebenezer
Angas Downs
Erldunda
Kulgera
Finke
Mulga Park
Bloods Range
Petermann Ranges
Mann Range
Murray Range
Tomkinson Range
Musgrave Range
Mount Woodroffe 1440
Mount Whinham
Birksgate Range
Everard Range
Fregon
Indulkana
Marla
Lake Maurice
Ooldea Range
Maralinga
Ooldea
Mulgathing
Wynbring
Hughes
Cook
Tarcoola
Nullarbor National Park
Colona
Penong
Fowlers Bay
Nuyts Archipelago
Ceduna
Streaky Bay
Point Kenny
Anxious Bay
Investigator Group
Lambert Azimuthal Equal Area Projection
1:13 000 000
miles
km

PAPUA NEW GUINEA
PORT MORESBY
SOLOMON ISLANDS
HONIARA
Guadalcanal
Rennell
Indispensable Reefs
VANUATU
Coral Sea
Coral Sea Islands Territory
(Australia)
Willis Group
Herald Cays
Magdelaine Cays
Diamond Islets
Flinders Reefs
Osprey Reef
Marion Reef
Saumarez Reef
Îles Chesterfield
(France)
Great Barrier Reef
Gulf of Carpentaria
Cape York Peninsula
Torres Strait
Thursday Island
Cape York
Cape Melville
Cairns
Townsville
Mackay
Rockhampton
Gladstone
Bundaberg
Fraser Island
Tropic of Capricorn
Sandy Cape
QUEENSLAND
Mount Isa
Longreach
Charleville
Toowoomba
Brisbane
Gold Coast
Darling Downs
Great Dividing Range
Simpson Desert
Lake Eyre
Sturt Stony Desert
PACIFIC OCEAN
NEW SOUTH WALES
Broken Hill
Dubbo
Newcastle
Sydney
Wollongong
Canberra
JERVIS BAY TERR.
Lord Howe Island
(Australia)
Tasman Sea
VICTORIA
Melbourne
Bendigo
Ballarat
Geelong
Adelaide
Port Augusta
Kangaroo Island
Spencer Gulf
Bass Strait
King Island
Flinders Island
Furneaux Group
Wilson's Promontory
TASMANIA
Launceston
Hobart
Devonport
Tasman Pen.
South East Cape

oceania

southeast australia

1:5 000 000

Conic Equidistant Projection

1:5 250 000

0 50 100 150 miles

0 50 100 150 200 250 km

Lambert Conformal Conic Projection

1:16 000 000

0 200 400 miles

0 200 400 600 800 km

Greenland
(Kalaallit Nunaat)
(Denmark)
Nationalparken i Nord- og Østgrønland
ICELAND
REYKJAVÍK
Denmark Strait
Baffin Bay
Davis Strait
Labrador Sea
Hudson Bay
James Bay
Hudson Strait
Foxe Basin
Foxe Channel
Gulf of Boothia
Queen Elizabeth Islands
Parry Islands
Ellesmere Island
Axel Heiberg Island
Devon Island
Cornwallis Island
Bathurst Island
Melville Island
Somerset Island
Prince of Wales Island
Baffin Island
Southampton Island
Coats Island
Mansel Island
Belcher Islands
Akimiski Island
Nottingham Island
Resolution Island
Cape Chidley
Péninsule d'Ungava
Melville Peninsula
Boothia Peninsula
Foxe Peninsula
Hall Peninsula
Cumberland Peninsula
Meta Incognita Peninsula
North Magnetic Pole (2000)
North Geomagnetic Pole (2000)
Nares Strait
Lancaster Sound
Jones Sound
Labrador
Newfoundland
NUNAVUT
MANITOBA
ONTARIO
QUÉBEC
NEWFOUNDLAND AND LABRADOR
NEW BRUNSWICK
NOVA SCOTIA
PRINCE EDWARD I.
St Pierre and Miquelon (France)
Île d'Anticosti
Gulf of St Lawrence
Cabot Strait
Sable Island
Bay of Fundy
Gulf of Maine
ATLANTIC OCEAN
NUUK (Godthåb)
Iqaluit
OTTAWA
Montréal
Québec
Toronto
Winnipeg
Halifax
St John's
Fredericton
Charlottetown
Thunder Bay
Sudbury
Lake Superior
Lake Michigan
Lake Huron
Lake Erie
L. Ontario
Lake Winnipeg
Lake Nipigon
MINNESOTA
WISCONSIN
MICHIGAN
IOWA
PENNSYLVANIA
NEW YORK
MAINE
Minneapolis
Chicago
Detroit
Cleveland
Buffalo
Boston
New York
Providence
AMERICA
NADA
Administrative divisions in the U.S.A. numbered on the map:
1. CONNECTICUT (K5)
2. MASSACHUSETTS (K5)
3. NEW HAMPSHIRE (K5)
4. RHODE ISLAND (K5)
5. VERMONT (K5)

→ 46

1:12 000 000

0 100 200 300 400 miles

0 100 200 300 400 500 600 700 km

CANADA
ONTARIO
QUÉBEC
NEW BRUNSWICK
NOVA SCOTIA
PRINCE EDWARD ISLAND
James Bay
Gulf of St Lawrence
Bay of Fundy
Gulf of Maine
Lake Superior
Lake Michigan
Lake Huron
Lake Erie
Lake Ontario
Georgian Bay
UNITED STATES OF AMERICA
MINNESOTA
WISCONSIN
MICHIGAN
IOWA
ILLINOIS
INDIANA
OHIO
PENNSYLVANIA
NEW YORK
VERMONT
NEW HAMPSHIRE
MAINE
MASSACHUSETTS
CONNECTICUT
RHODE ISLAND
NEW JERSEY
DELAWARE
MARYLAND
WEST VIRGINIA
VIRGINIA
KENTUCKY
MISSOURI
ARKANSAS
TENNESSEE
NORTH CAROLINA
SOUTH CAROLINA
GEORGIA
ALABAMA
MISSISSIPPI
LOUISIANA
FLORIDA
Appalachian Mountains
Allegheny Mountains
Cumberland Plateau
Ozark Plateau
Coastal Plain
Monts Notre Dame
ATLANTIC OCEAN
Gulf of Mexico
Straits of Florida
Great Bahama Bank
THE BAHAMAS
CUBA
Tropic of Cancer
OTTAWA
WASHINGTON
New York
Chicago
Philadelphia
Boston
Montréal
Toronto
Detroit
Atlanta
Miami
Houston
New Orleans
Jacksonville
NASSAU

Lambert Conformal Conic Projection

north america

northeast united states

1:3 500 000

0 50 100 miles

0 50 100 150 200 km

1:3 500 000

miles: 0 50 100
km: 0 50 100 150 200

north america
southwest united states

Lambert Conformal Conic Projection

→ 50

1:14 000 000

0 200 400 miles

0 200 400 600 800 km

ATLANTIC OCEAN
Caribbean Sea
West Indies
Greater Antilles
Lesser Antilles
Leeward Islands
Windward Islands
THE BAHAMAS
CUBA
HAITI
DOMINICAN REPUBLIC
JAMAICA
Puerto Rico (U.S.A.)
Bermuda (U.K.)
HAMILTON
Turks and Caicos Islands (U.K.)
Cayman Islands (U.K.)
Hispaniola
HAVANA (La Habana)
NASSAU
KINGSTON
PORT-AU-PRINCE
SANTO DOMINGO
SAN JUAN
ANTIGUA AND BARBUDA
ST KITTS AND NEVIS
DOMINICA
ST LUCIA
BARBADOS
ST VINCENT AND THE GRENADINES
GRENADA
TRINIDAD AND TOBAGO
Aruba (Neth.)
Netherlands Antilles
Guadeloupe (France)
Martinique (France)
VENEZUELA
COLOMBIA
GUYANA
BRAZIL
PANAMA
COSTA RICA
NICARAGUA
CARACAS
BOGOTÁ
PANAMA CITY
MANAGUA
SAN JOSÉ
Gulf of Panama
Straits of Florida
Great Bahama Bank
Tropic of Cancer
VIRGINIA
NORTH CAROLINA
SOUTH CAROLINA
GEORGIA
FLORIDA
Miami
Orlando
Tampa
Jacksonville
Atlanta
Charleston

Lambert Azimuthal Equal Area Projection

→ 52

1:14 000 000 — 0, 200, 400 miles; 0, 200, 400, 600, 800 km

south america

northern south america

Lambert Azimuthal Equal Area Projection

south america

southern south america

1:14 000 000

0 200 400 miles

0 200 400 600 800 km

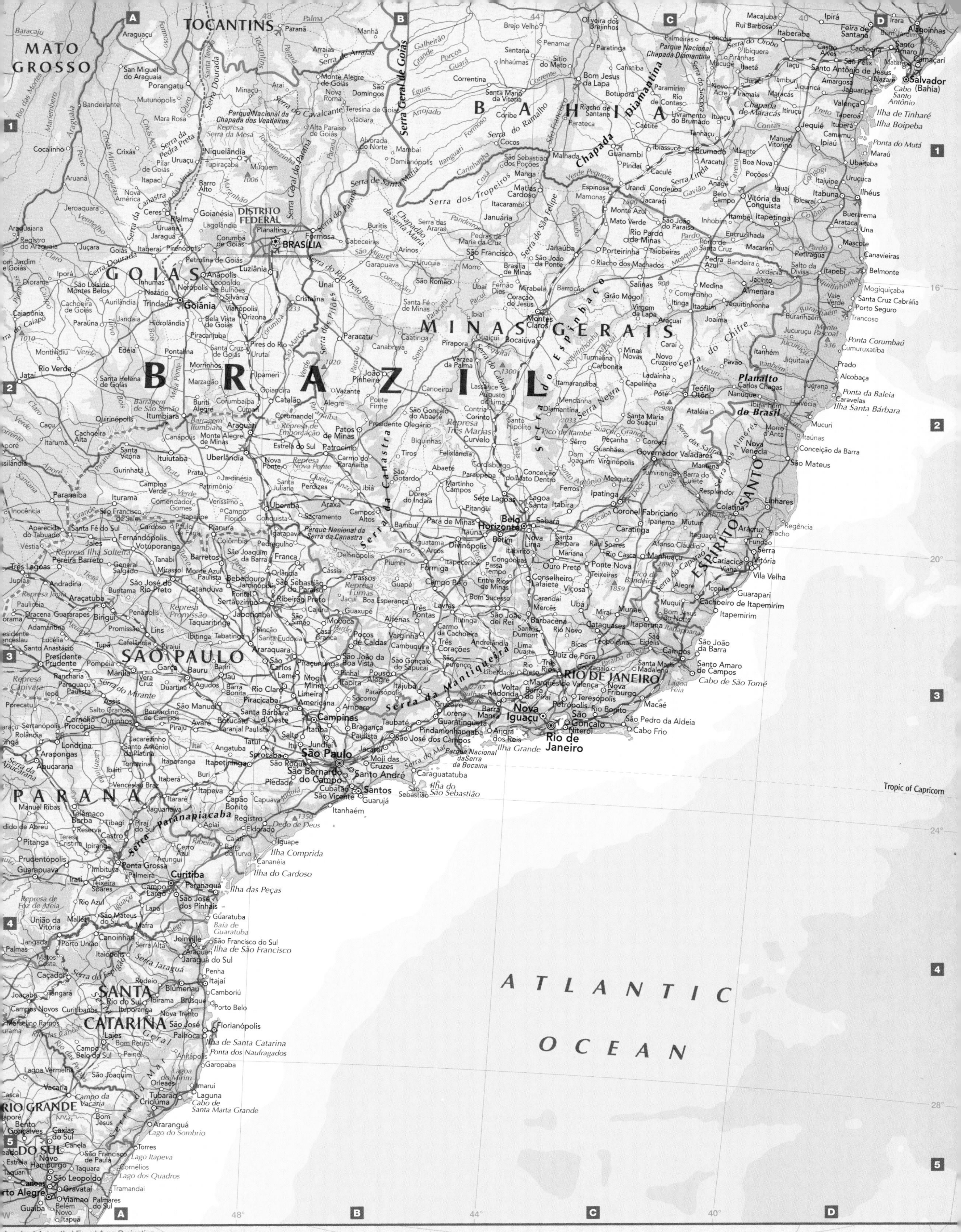

Lambert Azimuthal Equal Area Projection

1:7 000 000

0 100 200 miles

0 100 200 300 400 km

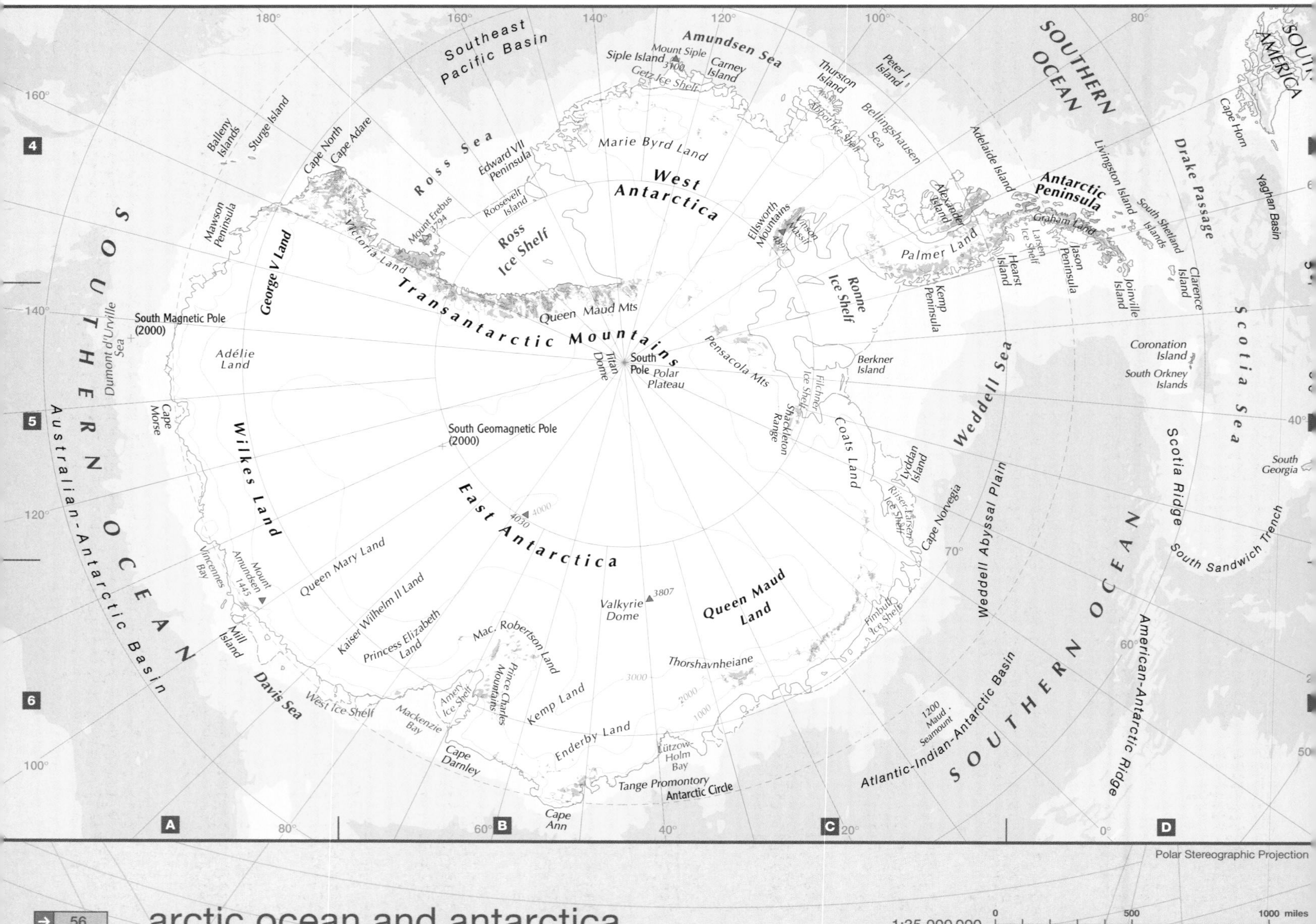

Polar Stereographic Projection

1:35 000 000

0 500 1000 miles

0 500 1000 1500 km

INDEX

The index includes the most significant names on the maps in the atlas. The names are generally indexed to the largest scale map on which they appear. For large physical features this will be the largest scale map on which they appear in their entirety or in the majority. Names can be located using the grid reference letters and numbers around the edges of the map. Names located on insets have a symbol □.

Abbreviations used to describe features in the index:

admin. dist.	administrative district
admin. div.	administrative division
admin. reg.	administrative region
aut. reg.	autonomous region
aut. rep.	autonomous republic
b.	bay
c.	cape
depr.	depression
des.	desert
esc.	escarpment
est.	estuary
for.	forest
g.	gulf
hd.	headland
i.	island
imp. lake	impermanent lake
is	islands
l.	lake
lag.	lagoon
mt.	mountain
mts	mountains
pen.	peninsula
plat.	plateau
pref.	prefecture
prov.	province
pt	point
r.	river
r. mouth	river mouth
reg.	region
resr.	reservoir
salt l.	salt lake
sea chan.	sea channel
terr.	territory
vol.	volcano

C

D

29F8 Dampier, Selat *sea chan.*
32C4 Danané
29C6 Đa Năng
48E2 Danbury
31B4 Dandong
50G5 Dangriga
22I4 Danilov
23J6 Danilovka
23H5 Dankov
51G6 Danlí
32C3 Dano
23F7 Danube *r.*
47J3 Danville
47L4 Danville
48C2 Danville
32C4 Daoukro
32D3 Dapaong
27J3 Da Qaidam Zhen
30B3 Daqing
32B3 Dara
33G1 Dar'ā
26E4 Dārāb
32E3 Darazo
21L4 Dardanelles *strait*
35D4 Dar es Salaam
43D2 Dargaville
27J2 Darhan
52C2 Darién, Golfo del *g.*
27H4 Darjiling
42B3 Darling *r.*
42D1 Darling Downs *hills*
40D6 Darling Range *hills*
14F4 Darlington
13L6 Darmstadt
33F1 Darnah
19F3 Daroca
22J4 Darovskoy
15H7 Dartford
15C8 Dartmoor *hills*
15D8 Dartmouth
45L5 Dartmouth
38E2 Daru
14E5 Darwen
40G2 Darwin
26E2 Dashoguz
23J8 Daşkäsän
21L5 Datça
30F4 Date
27K2 Datong
11N8 Daugava *r.*
11O9 Daugavpils
29E7 Davao
47I3 Davenport
15F6 Daventry
37I4 Daveyton
51H7 David
49I1 Davis
45M3 Davis Strait
26E5 Dawqah
44F4 Dawson Creek
18D5 Dax
42B6 Daylesford
33H1 Dayr az Zawr
47K4 Dayton
47K6 Daytona Beach
27J3 Dazhou
33G1 Dead Sea *salt l.*
15I7 Deal
15E7 Dean, Forest of
54D4 Deán Funes
14F5 Dearne *r.*
49D2 Death Valley *depr.*
15H9 Deauville
21I4 Debar
21I1 Debrecen
34D3 Debre Zeyit
47J4 Decatur
47J5 Decatur
27G5 Deccan *plat.*
42F1 Deception Bay
13O5 Děčín
47I3 Decorah
32C3 Dédougou
22F4 Dedovichi
14D5 Dee *est.*
15D5 Dee *r.*
16G3 Dee *r.*
32D4 Degema
13N6 Deggendorf
33H1 Dehlorān
21J1 Dej
47J3 De Kalb
34B3 Dékoa
7 Delap-Uliga-Djarrit
37G4 Delareyville
48D3 Delaware *r.*
48D3 Delaware *state*
48D3 Delaware Bay
18H3 Delémont
12E4 Delft
13K4 Delfzijl
27G4 Delhi
19H5 Dellys
49D4 Del Mar
13L4 Delmenhorst
20F2 Delnice
25Q2 De-Longa, Ostrova *is*
46G6 Del Rio
11J6 Delsbo
46F4 Delta
35C4 Demba
23F6 Demidov
46F5 Deming
21M5 Demirci
21L4 Demirköy
33H3 Denakil *reg.*
14D5 Denbigh
27J2 Dengkou
12J4 Den Helder
19G4 Denia
47H3 Denison
21M6 Denizli
42E4 Denman
11F8 Denmark
45P3 Denmark Strait
16F4 Denny
29D8 Denpasar
47H5 Denton
40D6 D'Entrecasteaux, Point
41K1 D'Entrecasteaux Islands
46F4 Denver
48C2 Denver
25O3 Deputatskiy
27G3 Dera Ghazi Khan
15F6 Derby
48E2 Derby
17D5 Derg, Lough *l.*
23K6 Dergachi
23H6 Derhachi
47I5 De Ridder
48F1 Derry
36F7 De Rust
14F6 Derwent *r.*
14G5 Derwent *r.*
26F1 Derzhavinsk
34D2 Desē
47I3 Des Moines
23F6 Desna *r.*
23G5 Desnogorsk
13N5 Dessau
35C5 Dete
13L5 Detmold
47K3 Detroit
47H2 Detroit Lakes
13O7 Deutschlandsberg
21J2 Deva
13K4 Deventer
46H2 Devil's Lake
15F7 Devizes
21L3 Devnya
45I2 Devon Island
41J8 Devonport
21N4 Devrek
27G4 Dewas
14F5 Dewsbury
27J3 Deyang
33H1 Dezfūl
25T3 Dezhneva, Mys *c.*
27K3 Dezhou
34F1 Dhahran
27I4 Dhaka
34E2 Dhamār
27H4 Dhanbad
32B3 Dhar Adrar *hills*
32C3 Dhar Oualâta *hills*
32C3 Dhar Tîchît *hills*
27G5 Dharwad
27G4 Dhule
34E3 Dhuusa Marreeb
49B2 Diablo, Mount
49B2 Diablo Range *mts*
54D4 Diamante
55C2 Diamantina
55C1 Diamantina, Chapada *plat.*
53G6 Diamantino
53I6 Dianópolis
32D3 Diapaga
35C4 Dibaya
27I4 Dibrugarh
46G2 Dickinson
32C3 Didiéni
32C3 Diébougou
32C3 Diéma
15I9 Dieppe
18I3 Dietikon
32E3 Diffa
18H4 Digne-les-Bains
18G3 Dijon
34E2 Dikhil
21L5 Dikili
24J2 Dikson
34D3 Dīla
29E8 Dili
44C4 Dillingham
46E2 Dillon
35C5 Dilolo
27I4 Dimapur
32C4 Dimbokro
21K3 Dimitrovgrad
23K5 Dimitrovgrad
18C2 Dinan
12J5 Dinant
21N5 Dinar
20G2 Dinaric Alps *mts*
27G5 Dindigul
17B5 Dingle Bay
32B3 Dinguiraye
16E3 Dingwall
32C3 Dioïla
54F3 Dionísio Cerqueira
32B3 Diourbel
29E7 Dipolog
32C3 Diré
34E3 Dirē Dawa
40C5 Dirk Hartog Island
34E2 Dīrs
41I7 Discovery Bay
55B1 Distrito Federal *admin. dist.*
36F5 Ditloung
55B3 Divinópolis
23I7 Divnoye
32C4 Divo
49B1 Dixon
44E4 Dixon Entrance *sea chan.*
26D3 Diyarbakır
32E2 Djado, Plateau du
34B4 Djambala
19H6 Djelfa
32C3 Djenné
32C3 Djibo
34E2 Djibouti
34E2 Djibouti *country*
32D4 Djougou
32E4 Djoum
23G5 Dmitriyev-L'govskiy
22H4 Dmitrov
26C2 Dnieper *r.*
23F7 Dniester *r.*
23G6 Dniprodzerzhyns'k
23G6 Dnipropetrovs'k
22F4 Dno
33E4 Doba
11M8 Dobele
29F8 Doberai, Jazirah *pen.*
20H2 Doboj
21L3 Dobrich
23I5 Dobrinka
23H5 Dobroye
23F5 Dobrush
21L7 Dodecanese *is*
46G4 Dodge City
35D4 Dodoma
32D3 Dogondoutchi
21M6 Doğu Menteşe Dağları *mts*
34F1 Doha
13J4 Dokkum
11O9 Dokshytsy
23H7 Dokuchayevs'k
18G3 Dole
15D6 Dolgellau
23H5 Dolgorukovo
30F3 Dolinsk
20D2 Dolomites *mts*
54E4 Dolores
54E5 Dolores
23D6 Dolyna
13N6 Domažlice
20H1 Dombóvár
54B3 Domeyko
51L5 Dominica
51J5 Dominican Republic
21J5 Domokos
29D8 Dompu
16G3 Don *r.*
23H7 Don *r.*
17G3 Donaghadee
42A6 Donald
19D4 Don Benito
14F5 Doncaster
35B4 Dondo
12D3 Donegal
17D3 Donegal Bay
23H7 Donets'k
23H6 Donets'kyy Kryazh *hills*
27J4 Dongchuan
27J5 Dongfang
31B5 Donggang
29C6 Đông Hơi
30C3 Dongning
33G3 Dongola
27K4 Dongting Hu *l.*
19F2 Donostia - San Sebastián
23I7 Donskoye
41H3 Doomadgee
15E8 Dorchester
18D4 Dordogne *r.*
12J5 Dordrecht
55B2 Dores do Indaiá
32C3 Dori
15G7 Dorking
16E3 Dornoch Firth *est.*
32C3 Doro
23G5 Dorogobuzh
23E7 Dorohoi
42F3 Dorrigo
13K5 Dortmund
32D3 Dosso
47J5 Dothan
18F1 Douai
32D4 Douala
43A7 Doubtful Sound *inlet*
32C3 Douentza
14C4 Douglas
46F3 Douglas
47K5 Douglas
52F4 Dourados
19B3 Douro *r.*
15I7 Dover
48A2 Dover
48D2 Dover
48D3 Dover
48F1 Dover
15I8 Dover, Strait of
17G3 Downpatrick
48D2 Doylestown
55A3 Dracena
13K4 Drachten
21K2 Drăgănești-Olt
21K2 Drăgășani
18H5 Draguignan
11N10 Drahichyn
37I3 Drakensberg *mts*
21K4 Drama
11G7 Drammen
20H2 Drava *r.*
20B6 Dréan
13N5 Dresden
18E2 Dreux
21J2 Drobeta - Turnu Severin
17F4 Drogheda
23D6 Drohobych
15E6 Droitwich Spa
17F3 Dromore
14F5 Dronfield
45K5 Drummondville
11N10 Druskininkai
11O7 Druzhnaya Gorka
21K3 Dryanovo
55A3 Duartina
26E4 Dubai
45H3 Dubawnt Lake
42D4 Dubbo
17F4 Dublin
47K5 Dublin
22H4 Dubna
23E6 Dubno
23I6 Dubovka
23I7 Dubovskoye
20H3 Dubrovnik
23E6 Dubrovytsya
47I3 Dubuque
24J3 Dudinka
15E6 Dudley
32C4 Duékoué
19C3 Duero *r.*
18H4 Dufourspitze *mt.*
20G3 Dugi Rat
13K5 Duisburg
37H6 Dukathole
23K5 Dukhovnitskoye
21L3 Dulovo
47I2 Duluth
29E7 Dumaguete
27J6 Dumai
46G4 Dumas
16E5 Dumbarton
16F5 Dumfries
33G1 Dumyāț
13P7 Dunajská Streda
21H1 Dunakeszi
20H1 Dunaújváros
23E6 Dunayivtsi
46H5 Duncan
16F2 Duncansby Head
11M8 Dundaga
17F3 Dundalk
48C3 Dundalk
17F4 Dundalk Bay
48B1 Dundas
16G4 Dundee
37J5 Dundee
17G3 Dundonald
43C7 Dunedin
16F4 Dunfermline
17F3 Dungannon
17E5 Dungarvan
15H8 Dungeness *hd*
17F3 Dungiven
42E4 Dungog
34C3 Dungu
29C7 Dungun
30C4 Dunhua
18F1 Dunkirk
48B1 Dunkirk
17F4 Dún Laoghaire
48D2 Dunmore
17G3 Dunmurry
16F2 Dunnet Head
48B1 Dunnville
16G5 Duns
15G7 Dunstable
21J3 Dupnitsa
23G8 Durağan
19E2 Durango
46F4 Durango
46G7 Durango
47H5 Durant
54E4 Durazno
37J5 Durban
18F5 Durban-Corbières
36D7 Durbanville
14F4 Durham
47L4 Durham
21M1 Durlești
21H4 Durrës
15F7 Durrington
21M5 Dursunbey
27F3 Dushanbe
13K5 Düsseldorf
32D3 Dutse
32D3 Dutsin-Ma
27J4 Duyun
21N4 Düzce
27F4 Dwarka
23G5 Dyat'kovo
47J4 Dyersburg
15D6 Dyfi *r.*
23H6 Dymytrov
35E5 Dzaoudzi
22I4 Dzerzhinsk
23G7 Dzhankoy
26F2 Dzhizak
26F2 Dzhusaly
13R4 Działdowo
27J2 Dzuunmod
11O10 Dzyarzhynsk

E

46G6 Eagle Pass
16E4 Earn, Loch *l.*
15H8 Eastbourne
28E4 East China Sea
15H6 East Dereham
6 Easter Island
37H6 Eastern Cape *prov.*
33G2 Eastern Desert
27G5 Eastern Ghats *mts*
54E8 East Falkland *i.*
13K4 East Frisian Islands
15G7 East Grinstead
48E1 Easthampton
48E2 East Hartford
16E5 East Kilbride
48A2 Eastlake
15F8 Eastleigh
48A2 East Liverpool
37H7 East London
45K4 Eastmain *r.*
48C3 Easton
48D2 Easton
48D2 East Orange
48F2 East Providence
25P2 East Siberian Sea
29E8 East Timor
48B1 East York
47I3 Eau Claire
15D7 Ebbw Vale
32E4 Ebebiyin
13N4 Eberswalde-Finow
30F4 Ebetsu
20F4 Eboli
32E4 Ebolowa
19G3 Ebro *r.*
19G5 Ech Chélif
19D5 Écija
13L3 Eckernförde
52C4 Ecuador
33H3 Ed
16G1 Eday *i.*
33G3 Ed Damazin
33G3 Ed Damer
33G3 Ed Dueim
32E4 Edéa
55A2 Edéia
42D6 Eden
17E4 Edenderry
21J4 Edessa
46H6 Edinburg
16F5 Edinburgh
21L4 Edirne
44G4 Edmonton
45L5 Edmundston
21L5 Edremit
34C4 Edward, Lake
46G5 Edwards Plateau
47J4 Effingham
13R7 Eger
11E7 Egersund
10□1 Egilsstaðir
21N6 Eğirdir
43D4 Egmont, Cape
25T3 Egvekinot
33G2 Egypt
27J3 Ehen Hudag
13L6 Ehingen (Donau)
13K5 Eifel *hills*
16C4 Eigg *i.*
40E3 Eighty Mile Beach
33G2 Eilat
12J5 Eindhoven
18I3 Einsiedeln
52E5 Eirunepé
13M5 Eisenach
13O4 Eisenhüttenstadt
13P7 Eisenstadt
11M7 Ekenäs
27G1 Ekibastuz
11I8 Eksjö
20B6 El Aouinet
20B6 El Arrouch
26C3 Elazığ
20D3 Elba, Isola d' *i.*
30E2 El'ban
21I4 Elbasan
32D1 El Bayadh
13L4 Elbe *r.*
46F4 Elbert, Mount
15I9 Elbeuf
13Q3 Elbląg
23I8 El'brus *mt.*
26D3 Elburz Mountains
49D4 El Cajon
52F2 El Callao
47H6 El Campo
49E4 El Centro
52F7 El Cerro
19F4 Elche-Elx
19F4 Elda
25O3 El'dikan
47H4 El Dorado
47H5 El Dorado
54F3 Eldorado
55A4 Eldorado
34D3 Eldoret
19E5 El Ejido
34D3 Elemi Triangle *terr.*
47L6 Eleuthera *i.*
33F3 El Fasher
46F6 El Fuerte
33F3 El Geneina
16F3 Elgin
47J3 Elgin
32D1 El Goléa
26C6 Elgon, Mount
20B6 El Hadjar
32C2 El Hank *esc.*
51J5 Elías Piña
23J7 Elista
48D2 Elizabeth
47L4 Elizabeth City
47J4 Elizabethtown
32C1 El Jadida
20D7 El Jem
13R4 Ełk
20C6 El Kala
46H4 Elk City
32C1 El Kelaâ des Srarhna
46E1 Elkford
49B1 Elk Grove
47J3 Elkhart
21L3 Elkhovo
48B3 Elkins
46D3 Elko
48D3 Elkton
46C2 Ellensburg
45J2 Ellesmere Island
14E5 Ellesmere Port
48C3 Ellicott City
37H6 Elliot
47N3 Ellsworth
21M6 Elmalı
32D1 El Meghaïer
48C1 Elmira
13L4 Elmshorn
33F3 El Muglad
32D1 El Oued
46F5 El Paso
46F5 El Porvenir
51I7 El Porvenir
19H3 El Prat de Llobregat
50G5 El Progreso
19C5 El Puerto de Santa María
46H4 El Reno
46F7 El Salto
54C3 El Salvador
50G6 El Salvador *country*
49D4 Elsinore
20C6 El Tarf
52F2 El Tigre
23J6 El'ton
19C4 Elvas
11G6 Elverum
15H6 Ely
47K3 Elyria
26E2 Emba
37I4 Embalenhle
54D2 Embarcación
34D4 Embu
13K4 Emden
21M5 Emet
37J3 eMijindini
33E3 Emi Koussi *mt.*
50F5 Emiliano Zapata
21N5 Emirdağ
11I8 Emmaboda
48D2 Emmaus
13K4 Emmen
18I3 Emmen
37J5 Empangeni
20D3 Empoli
47H4 Emporia
47L4 Emporia
37I4 Emzinoni
54E3 Encarnación
49D4 Encinitas
55C1 Encruzilhada
41I2 Endeavour Strait
48C1 Endicott
23G7 Enerhodar
23J6 Engel's
15E6 England *admin. div.*
15F9 English Channel
46H4 Enid
30F4 Eniwa
11J7 Enköping
20F6 Enna
17D5 Ennis
47H5 Ennis
17F5 Enniscorthy
17E3 Enniskillen
13K4 Enschede
46D6 Ensenada
27J3 Enshi
34D3 Entebbe
55B3 Entre Rios de Minas
19B4 Entroncamento
32D4 Enugu
52D5 Envira
48C2 Ephrata
18H2 Épinal
15G7 Epsom
32D4 Equatorial Guinea
20H1 Érd
21L4 Erdek
54F3 Erechim
21N4 Ereğli
21N6 Ereğli
27K2 Erenhot
13M5 Erfurt
32C2 'Erg Chech *des.*
11N8 Ērgļi
48A1 Erie
48A1 Erie, Lake
34D2 Eritrea
13M6 Erlangen
37I4 Ermelo
21K6 Ermoupoli
27G5 Erode
36B1 Erongo *admin. reg.*
32C1 Er Rachidia
23I6 Ertil'
13N5 Erzgebirge *mts*
26C3 Erzincan
26D3 Erzurum
11F9 Esbjerg
47J2 Escanaba
50F5 Escárcega
13M5 Eschwege
49D4 Escondido
50C4 Escuinapa
50F5 Escuintla
32E4 Eséka
26E3 Eşfahān
37J5 Esikhawini
11J7 Eskilstuna
23G8 Eskipazar
21N5 Eskişehir
33H1 Eslāmābād-e Gharb
11H9 Eslöv
21M5 Eşme
52C3 Esmeraldas
40E6 Esperance
46F6 Esperanza
55C2 Espinhaço, Serra do *mts*
55C1 Espinosa
55C2 Espírito Santo *state*
39G3 Espíritu Santo *i.*
11N6 Espoo
54B6 Esquel
32C1 Essaouira
32B2 Es Semara
13K5 Essen
53G2 Essequibo *r.*
48C3 Essex
53K6 Estância
37I5 Estcourt
51G6 Estelí
19D5 Estepona
46G2 Estevan
47I3 Estherville
11N7 Estonia
55A5 Estrela
19C3 Estrela, Serra da *mts*
55B2 Estrela do Sul
19C4 Estremoz
18F2 Étampes
37J4 eThandakukhanya
34D3 Ethiopia
20F6 Etna, Mount *vol.*
48B1 Etobicoke
35B5 Etosha Pan *salt pan*
48A2 Euclid
53K6 Euclides da Cunha
46C3 Eugene
26D3 Euphrates *r.*
11M6 Eura
46C3 Eureka
46D2 Eureka
42B6 Euroa
35E6 Europa, Île *i.*
19D5 Europa Point
48A2 Evans City
46E3 Evanston
47J4 Evansville
37H4 Evaton
40G5 Everard Range *hills*
27H4 Everest, Mount
46C2 Everett
47K6 Everglades *swamp*
15F6 Evesham
19C4 Évora
18E2 Évreux
21K5 Evvoia *i.*
16D3 Ewe, Loch *b.*
34B4 Ewo
15D8 Exe *r.*
15D8 Exeter
15D7 Exmoor *hills*
15D8 Exmouth
40C4 Exmouth
40C4 Exmouth Gulf
48D2 Exton
19D4 Extremadura *reg.*
34D4 Eyasi, Lake *salt l.*
16G5 Eyemouth
10□1 Eyjafjörður *inlet*
15F7 Eynsham
41H5 Eyre (North), Lake *salt flat*
41H6 Eyre Peninsula
41H5 Eyre (South), Lake *salt flat*
37J5 Ezakheni
22K3 Ezhva
21L5 Ezine

F

11G9 Fåborg
20E3 Fabriano
32D3 Fada-N'Gourma
20D2 Faenza
21K2 Făgăraș
39I3 Fagatogo
11I7 Fagersta
44D3 Fairbanks
48C3 Fairfax
49A1 Fairfield
17F2 Fair Head
16H1 Fair Isle *i.*
47I3 Fairmont
48A3 Fairmont
27G3 Faisalabad
22K4 Falenki
11H8 Falkenberg
16F5 Falkirk
54E8 Falkland Islands *terr.*
54D8 Falkland Sound *sea chan.*
11H7 Falköping
49D4 Fallbrook
46D4 Fallon
48F2 Fall River
15B8 Falmouth
48F2 Falmouth
36D8 False Bay
11G9 Falster *i.*
23E7 Fălticeni
11I6 Falun
33G1 Famagusta
35E6 Fandriana
30C3 Fangzheng
20E3 Fano
32B3 Faraba
35E6 Farafangana
33F2 Farāfirah, Wāḥāt al *oasis*
26F3 Farāh
32B3 Faranah
15F8 Fareham
43D5 Farewell, Cape
45N3 Farewell, Cape
47H2 Fargo
47I3 Faribault
46F4 Farmington
48B4 Farmville
15G7 Farnborough
15G7 Farnham
19C5 Faro
53G4 Faro
10□2 Faroe Islands *terr.*
35F5 Farquhar Group *is*
11E7 Farsund
20G4 Fasano
23F6 Fastiv
27H4 Fatehpur
32B3 Fatick
10I3 Fauske
15F8 Fawley
10□1 Faxaflói *b.*
33E3 Faya
47I4 Fayetteville
47L4 Fayetteville
32B2 Fdérik
47L5 Fear, Cape
18E2 Fécamp
48D3 Federalsburg
52D5 Feijó
55D1 Feira de Santana
13L7 Feldkirch
13O7 Feldkirchen in Kärnten
50G5 Felipe C. Puerto
55B2 Felixlândia
15I7 Felixstowe
35E5 Fenoarivo Atsinanana
23G7 Feodosiya
21L4 Feres
47H2 Fergus Falls
20C7 Fériana
32C4 Ferkessédougou
20E3 Fermo
19C3 Fermoselle
47K5 Fernandina Beach
55A3 Fernandópolis
20D2 Ferrara
19B2 Ferrol
55C2 Ferros
32C1 Fès
21M6 Fethiye
16□ Fetlar *i.*
27G3 Feyzābād
15D6 Ffestiniog
35E6 Fianarantsoa
21H4 Fier
16G4 Fife Ness *pt*
18F4 Figeac
19B3 Figueira da Foz
19H2 Figueres
32C1 Figuig
33E4 Figuil
39I3 Fiji
54D2 Filadelfia
14G4 Filey
32D3 Filingué
21I5 Filippiada
11I7 Filipstad
49C3 Fillmore
47K3 Findlay
48C1 Finger Lakes
21N6 Finike
19B2 Finisterre, Cape
11O5 Finland
11M7 Finland, Gulf of
10H2 Finnmarksvidda *reg.*
11I7 Finspång
54D4 Firmat
18G4 Firminy
36C5 Fish *watercourse*
45J3 Fisher Strait
15C7 Fishguard
37I6 Flagstaff
46E4 Flagstaff
14G4 Flamborough Head
46C2 Flattery, Cape
14D5 Fleetwood
11E7 Flekkefjord
11J7 Flen
13L3 Flensburg
41J7 Flinders Island
41H6 Flinders Ranges *mts*
44H4 Flin Flon
14D5 Flint
47K3 Flint
20D3 Florence
46E5 Florence
47J5 Florence
47L5 Florence
52C3 Florencia
53G5 Flores
29E8 Flores *i.*
29D8 Flores, Laut *sea*
53K5 Floresta
53J5 Floriano
55A4 Florianópolis
54E4 Florida
47K5 Florida *state*
47K7 Florida, Straits of
49B1 Florin
21I4 Florina
11D6 Florø
21L5 Foça
21L2 Focșani
20F4 Foggia
18E5 Foix
10I3 Folda *sea chan.*
20E3 Foligno
15I7 Folkestone
20D3 Follonica
35E5 Fomboni
47J3 Fond du Lac
20E4 Fondi
52E4 Fonte Boa
10□1 Fontur *pt*
44C3 Foraker, Mount
13M6 Forchheim
15H6 Fordham
15F8 Fordingbridge
32B4 Forécariah
47J5 Forest
42C5 Forest Hill
49A1 Forestville
16G4 Forfar
48D3 Forked River
20E2 Forlì
14D5 Formby
55B3 Formiga
54E3 Formosa
55B1 Formosa
55A1 Formoso *r.*
47I4 Forrest City
11M6 Forssa
42F4 Forster
53K4 Fortaleza
51L6 Fort-de-France
47I3 Fort Dodge
48E1 Fort Edward
16F4 Forth *r.*
16F4 Forth, Firth of *est.*
47K6 Fort Lauderdale
46E2 Fort Macleod
44G4 Fort McMurray
47K6 Fort Myers
47J5 Fort Payne
47K6 Fort Pierce
34D3 Fort Portal
47I4 Fort Scott
44G3 Fort Smith
47I4 Fort Smith
46G5 Fort Stockton
47J3 Fort Wayne
16D4 Fort William
47H5 Fort Worth
20B2 Fossano
42C7 Foster
18D2 Fougères
16□ Foula *i.*
32E4 Foumban
32B3 Fouta Djallon *reg.*
43A8 Foveaux Strait
46G4 Fowler
44G4 Fox Creek
45K3 Foxe Basin *g.*
17E3 Foyle *r.*
17E2 Foyle, Lough *b.*
54F3 Foz do Iguaçu
48F1 Framingham
55B3 Franca
20G4 Francavilla Fontana
18F3 France
34B4 Franceville
35C6 Francistown
47K4 Frankfort
13L5 Frankfurt am Main
13O4 Frankfurt an der Oder
13M6 Fränkische Alb *hills*
48B2 Franklin
48F1 Franklin
46D2 Franklin D. Roosevelt Lake *resr*
42B7 Frankston
24G2 Frantsa-Iosifa, Zemlya *is*
20E4 Frascati
44F5 Fraser *r.*
45L4 Fraser *r.*
16G3 Fraserburgh
18I3 Frauenfeld
54E4 Fray Bentos
14E5 Freckleton
11F9 Fredericia
46H5 Frederick
48C3 Frederick
46H5 Fredericksburg
48C3 Fredericksburg
45L5 Fredericton
11G8 Frederikshavn
11H9 Frederiksværk
48B1 Fredonia
11G7 Fredrikstad
48D2 Freehold
47H6 Freeport
47L6 Freeport City
37H5 Free State *prov.*
32B4 Freetown
13K6 Freiburg im Breisgau
13M6 Freising
13O6 Freistadt
18H5 Fréjus
40D6 Fremantle
47H3 Fremont
49B2 Fremont
53H3 French Guiana *terr.*
6 French Polynesia *terr.*
7 French Southern and Antarctic Lands
19G6 Frenda
50D4 Fresnillo
49C2 Fresno
13L6 Freudenstadt
32B3 Fria
54C3 Frias
18H3 Fribourg
13L7 Friedrichshafen
45L3 Frobisher Bay
10F5 Frohavet *b.*
23I6 Frolovo
15E7 Frome
41H6 Frome, Lake *salt flat*
50F5 Frontera
46F6 Fronteras
48B3 Front Royal
20F4 Frosinone
13Q6 Frýdek-Místek
19E3 Fuenlabrada
54E2 Fuerte Olimpo
32B2 Fuerteventura *i.*
26E4 Fujairah
31E6 Fuji
30C3 Fujin
31E6 Fujinomiya
31E6 Fuji-san *vol.*
31E6 Fujiyoshida
31D6 Fukuchiyama
31E5 Fukui
31C6 Fukuoka
31F5 Fukushima
13L5 Fulda
49D4 Fullerton
47I4 Fulton
48C1 Fulton
31E6 Funabashi
39H2 Funafuti *atoll*
32B1 Funchal
19C3 Fundão
55C2 Fundão
45L5 Fundy, Bay of *g.*
32D3 Funtua
22I4 Furmanov
55B3 Furnas, Represa *resr*
41J8 Furneaux Group *is*
13O4 Fürstenwalde
13M6 Fürth
31F5 Furukawa
30A4 Fushun
30B4 Fusong
27K3 Fuyang
30B3 Fuyu
30B3 Fuyu
27H2 Fuyun
27K4 Fuzhou
28D5 Fuzhou
11G9 Fyn *i.*
16D5 Fyne, Loch *inlet*

G

34E3 Gaalkacyo
35B5 Gabela
32E1 Gabès
32E1 Gabès, Golfe de *g.*
34B4 Gabon
37G3 Gaborone
21K3 Gabrovo
32B3 Gabú
47J5 Gadsden
21K2 Găești
20E4 Gaeta
20C7 Gafsa
23G5 Gagarin
32C4 Gagnoa
23I8 Gagra
47H5 Gainesville
47K5 Gainesville
47K6 Gainesville
14G5 Gainsborough
41H6 Gairdner, Lake *salt flat*
13P6 Galanta
16G5 Galashiels
21M2 Galați
20H4 Galatina
47I3 Galesburg
36G5 Galeshewe
22I4 Galich
19C2 Galicia *reg.*
47J4 Gallatin
27H6 Galle
52D1 Gallinas, Punta *pt*
20H4 Gallipoli
21L4 Gallipoli
10L3 Gällivare
46F4 Gallup
17D5 Galtee Mountains *hills*
47I6 Galveston
47I6 Galveston Bay
17C4 Galway
17C4 Galway Bay
37J6 Gamalakhe
32B3 Gambia, The
34D3 Gambēla
34B4 Gamboma
11J8 Gamleby
23J8 Gäncä
35B5 Ganda
35C4 Gandajika
45M5 Gander
19G3 Gandesa
27G4 Gandhinagar
19F4 Gandía
27G4 Ganganagar
27H3 Gangdisê Shan *mts*
27I4 Ganges *r.*
27H4 Ganges, Mouths of the
30A3 Gannan
44H5 Gannett Peak
32E4 Ganye
32C3 Gao
32C3 Gaoua
32B3 Gaoual
18H4 Gap
32C3 Garalo
53K5 Garanhuns
37H3 Ga-Rankuwa
34E3 Garbahaarey
13L4 Garbsen
55A3 Garça
20D2 Garda, Lake
46G4 Garden City
27F3 Gardēz
48F1 Gardner
11L9 Gargždai
37G6 Gariep Dam *resr*
36C6 Garies
34D4 Garissa
18D4 Garonne *r.*
55A5 Garopaba
32E4 Garoua
47J3 Gary
46D6 Garza García
18D5 Gascony *reg.*
18C5 Gascony, Gulf of
40C5 Gascoyne *r.*
32E3 Gashua
47N2 Gaspé, Péninsule de *pen.*
47K4 Gastonia
11Q7 Gatchina
14F4 Gateshead
46H5 Gatesville
37I4 Gauteng *prov.*
21K7 Gavdos *i.*
11J6 Gävle
22H4 Gavrilov-Yam
41H6 Gawler
41H6 Gawler Ranges *hills*
32D3 Gaya
32D3 Gayéri
41K5 Gayndah
22L3 Gayny
33G1 Gaza
37K2 Gaza *prov.*
26C3 Gaziantep
32C4 Gbarnga
13Q3 Gdańsk
13Q3 Gdańsk, Gulf of
11O7 Gdov
13Q3 Gdynia
33G3 Gedaref
42B7 Geelong
11F6 Geilo
27J4 Gejiu
20F6 Gela
23H7 Gelendzhik
34B3 Gemena
21M4 Gemlik
54D5 General Acha
54C5 General Alvear
54E5 General Juan Madariaga
54D5 General Pico
54C5 General Roca
55A3 General Salgado
29E7 General Santos
54D5 General Villegas
48C1 Geneseo
18H3 Geneva
48C1 Geneva
18H3 Geneva, Lake
30A2 Genhe
13J5 Genk
20C2 Genoa
20C2 Genoa, Gulf of
40D6 Geographe Bay
40C4 Geographe Channel
36F7 George
29C7 George Town
32B3 Georgetown
46H5 Georgetown
47L5 Georgetown
51H5 George Town
53G2 Georgetown
23I8 Georgia
47K5 Georgia *state*
45J5 Georgian Bay
27H2 Georgiyevka
23I7 Georgiyevsk
13N5 Gera
55B1 Geral de Goiás, Serra *hills*
55B1 Geral do Paraná, Serra *hills*
40C5 Geraldton
23G8 Gerede
13L5 Germany
23G8 Gerze
48C3 Gettysburg
21J4 Gevgelija
21N4 Geyve
32D1 Ghadāmis
32C4 Ghana
35C6 Ghanzi
36F2 Ghanzi *admin. dist.*
32D1 Ghardaïa
33E1 Gharyān
33E3 Ghazal, Bahr el *watercourse*
19F6 Ghazaouet
27G4 Ghaziabad
26F3 Ghaznī
12I5 Ghent
21K1 Gheorgheni
21J1 Gherla
18I5 Ghisonaccia
23I7 Giaginskaya
21J4 Giannitsa
17F2 Giant's Causeway *lava field*
20F6 Giarre
19D5 Gibraltar *terr.*
19C6 Gibraltar, Strait of
40E4 Gibson Desert
13L5 Gießen
31E6 Gifu
19D2 Gijón-Xixón
49E4 Gila *r.*
53I5 Gilbués
42D3 Gilgandra
27G3 Gilgit
46F3 Gillette
15H7 Gillingham
49B2 Gilroy
20G4 Ginosa
20G4 Gioia del Colle
42B7 Gippsland *reg.*
23H8 Giresun
19H3 Girona
18D4 Gironde *est.*
16E5 Girvan
43G4 Gisborne
11H8 Gislaved
34C4 Gitarama
34C4 Gitega
20E3 Giulianova
21K3 Giurgiu
37J2 Giyani
33G2 Giza
21I4 Gjirokastër
11G6 Gjøvik
45M5 Glace Bay
41K4 Gladstone
20G2 Glamoč
16E5 Glasgow
47J4 Glasgow
15E7 Glastonbury
22L4 Glazov
46E5 Glendale
49C3 Glendale
42E2 Glen Innes
16E3 Glen More *valley*
16F4 Glenrothes
48E1 Glens Falls
13O5 Gliwice
46E5 Globe
13P5 Głogów
10H3 Glomfjord
15E7 Gloucester
42E3 Gloucester
48F1 Gloucester
48D1 Gloversville
23I6 Glubokiy
27H1 Glubokoye
13O6 Gmünd
13N7 Gmunden
13P4 Gniezno
21I3 Gnjilane
34E3 Goba
36D2 Gobabis
27J2 Gobi *des.*
31D6 Gobō
36D3 Gochas
15G7 Godalming
27H5 Godavari *r.*
53L5 Goiana
55A1 Goianésia
55A2 Goiânia
55A1 Goiás
55A2 Goiás *state*
54F2 Goio-Erê
21K4 Gökçeada *i.*
21M4 Gölcük
42F2 Gold Coast
43D5 Golden Bay
47L4 Goldsboro
23I8 Göle
49C3 Goleta
23H8 Gölköy
27I3 Golmud
21N4 Gölpazarı
34C4 Goma
32E3 Gombe
46G6 Gómez Palacio
51J5 Gonaïves
26E3 Gonbad-e Kavus
34D2 Gonder
21L4 Gönen
47H6 Gonzales
36D8 Good Hope, Cape of
14G5 Goole
42E2 Goondiwindi
13L6 Göppingen
27H4 Gorakhpur
21M5 Gördes
34D3 Gorē
17F5 Gorey
26E3 Gorgān
20E2 Gorizia
23D6 Gorlice
13O5 Görlitz
21K3 Gorna Oryakhovitsa
21I2 Gornji Milanovac
20G3 Gornji Vakuf
24J4 Gorno-Altaysk
30F3 Gornozavodsk
24J4 Gornyak
23K6 Gornyy
22I4 Gorodets
23J5 Gorodishche
23J6 Gorodishche
23I7 Gorodovikovsk
38E2 Goroka
22I4 Gorokhovets
32C3 Gorom Gorom
29E7 Gorontalo
23H6 Gorshechnoye
23H7 Goryachiy Klyuch
13O4 Gorzów Wielkopolski
14F3 Gosforth
48D2 Goshen
20F2 Gospić
15F8 Gosport
32C3 Gossi
21I4 Gostivar
11H7 Götene
13M5 Gotha
11G8 Gothenburg
11K8 Gotland *i.*
21J4 Gotse Delchev
31D6 Götsu
13L5 Göttingen
12J4 Gouda
45K5 Gouin, Réservoir
42D5 Goulburn
32C3 Goundam
19G5 Gouraya
32C3 Gourcy
32E3 Gouré
55C2 Governador Valadares
27I2 Govĭ Altayn Nuruu *mts*
54E3 Goya
23J8 Göyçay
20F6 Gozo *i.*
36G7 Graaf-Reinet
36D8 Grabouw
20F2 Gračac
42F2 Grafton
48A3 Grafton
46H5 Graham
37H7 Grahamstown
53I5 Grajaú
16E4 Grampian Mountains
19E5 Granada
51G6 Granada
45K5 Granby
32B2 Gran Canaria *i.*
54D3 Gran Chaco *reg.*
47L6 Grand Bahama *i.*
45M5 Grand Bank
45M5 Grand Banks of Newfoundland *sea feature*
32C4 Grand-Bassam
49F2 Grand Canyon *gorge*
51H5 Grand Cayman *i.*
54C8 Grande, Bahía *b.*
44G4 Grande Prairie
32E3 Grand Erg de Bilma *des.*
32C1 Grand Erg Occidental *des.*
32D2 Grand Erg Oriental *des.*
54C4 Grandes, Salinas *salt marsh*
45M5 Grand Falls
47H2 Grand Forks
46H3 Grand Island
46F4 Grand Junction
32C4 Grand-Lahou
19B4 Grândola
47I2 Grand Rapids
47J3 Grand Rapids
51J4 Grand Turk
11G6 Grängesberg
53J4 Granja
11I7 Gränna
15G6 Grantham
16F3 Grantown-on-Spey
46F4 Grants
46C3 Grants Pass
48C2 Grantville
55C2 Grão Mogol
37J3 Graskop
18H5 Grasse
19G2 Graus
55A5 Gravataí
15H7 Gravesend
20G4 Gravina in Puglia
15H7 Grays
13O7 Graz
47L6 Great Abaco *i.*
40F6 Great Australian Bight *g.*
47L6 Great Bahama Bank *sea feature*
43E3 Great Barrier Island
41I2 Great Barrier Reef
46D4 Great Basin
44G3 Great Bear Lake
11G9 Great Belt *sea chan.*
46H4 Great Bend
12G4 Great Britain *i.*
42B6 Great Dividing Range *mts*
51H4 Greater Antilles *is*
47L7 Great Exuma *i.*
46E2 Great Falls
47M7 Great Inagua *i.*
36F7 Great Karoo *plat.*
15E6 Great Malvern
27I6 Great Nicobar *i.*
15H6 Great Ouse *r.*
34D4 Great Rift Valley
46E3 Great Salt Lake
46E3 Great Salt Lake Desert
33F2 Great Sand Sea *des.*
40E4 Great Sandy Desert
44G3 Great Slave Lake
15I7 Great Stour *r.*
15C8 Great Torrington
40F5 Great Victoria Desert
15H7 Great Waltham
15I6 Great Yarmouth
48C1 Greece
21I5 Greece *country*
46G3 Greeley
47J3 Green Bay
47J2 Green Bay *b.*
47K4 Greeneville
48F1 Greenfield
45N2 Greenland *terr.*
24A2 Greenland Sea
16E5 Greenock
46F3 Green River
48B2 Greensburg
32C4 Greenville
47H5 Greenville
47I5 Greenville
47J5 Greenville
47K5 Greenville
48B2 Greenwich
47K5 Greenwood
40F4 Gregory, Lake *salt flat*
40E4 Gregory Range *hills*
41I3 Gregory Range *hills*
13N3 Greifswald
11G8 Grenå
47J5 Grenada
51L6 Grenada *country*
42D4 Grenfell
18G4 Grenoble
16F6 Gretna
21I4 Grevena
46F3 Greybull
43C6 Greymouth
42A2 Grey Range *hills*
23I6 Gribanovskiy
47K5 Griffin
42C5 Griffith
34C3 Grimari
14G5 Grimsby
44G4 Grimshaw
11F7 Grimstad
10□1 Grindavík
11F9 Grindsted
20G2 Grmeč *mts*
37I3 Groblersdal
30C3 Grodekovo
13K4 Groningen
41H2 Groote Eylandt *i.*
35B5 Grootfontein
36E7 Groot Swartberge *mts*
36E5 Grootvloer *salt pan*
20D3 Grosseto
13L6 Groß-Gerau
13N7 Großglockner *mt.*
49B3 Grover Beach
23J8 Groznyy
20G2 Grubišno Polje
13Q4 Grudziądz
23H5 Gryazi
22I4 Gryazovets
13O4 Gryfice
13O4 Gryfino
19B2 Guadalajara
50D4 Guadalajara
41M1 Guadalcanal *i.*
19C5 Guadalquivir *r.*
46G7 Guadalupe Victoria
19D3 Guadarrama, Sierra de *mts*
51L5 Guadeloupe *terr.*
19E5 Guadix
55A5 Guaíba
54F2 Guaíra
54E4 Gualeguay
54E4 Gualeguaychu
29G6 Guam *terr.*
46F6 Guamúchil
50D4 Guanajuato
55C1 Guanambi
52E2 Guanare
51H4 Guane
27J3 Guangyuan
27K4 Guangzhou
55C2 Guanhães
51I4 Guantánamo
55B3 Guapé
55A5 Guaporé
52E6 Guaporé *r.*
53K5 Guarabira
52C4 Guaranda
55C3 Guarapari
55A4 Guarapuava
55A3 Guararapes
55B3 Guaratinguetá
55A4 Guaratuba
19C3 Guarda
55B3 Guarujá
46F6 Guasave
50F5 Guatemala
50F6 Guatemala City
55B3 Guaxupé
52C4 Guayaquil
52B4 Guayaquil, Golfo de *g.*
46E6 Guaymas
23H6 Gubkin
23J8 Gudermes
32B4 Guéckédou
20B6 Guelma
32B2 Guelmine
48A1 Guelph
18E3 Guéret
15E9 Guernsey *terr.*
32B3 Guérou
52E2 Guiana Highlands *mts*
33E4 Guider
20E4 Guidonia-Montecelio
32C4 Guiglo
15G7 Guildford
27K4 Guilin
19B3 Guimarães
53J4 Guimarães
32B3 Guinea
32D4 Guinea, Gulf of
32B3 Guinea-Bissau
51H4 Güines
53H7 Guiratinga
27J4 Guiyang
27G3 Gujranwala
23H6 Gukovo
27G5 Gulbarga
11O8 Gulbene
47J5 Gulfport
27F2 Gulistan
23I7 Gul'kevichi
34D3 Gulu
35C5 Gumare
32D3 Gumel
27G4 Guna
42D5 Gundagai
21M5 Güney
46F4 Gunnison
27G5 Guntakal
29B7 Gunungsitoli
55A2 Gurinhatã
53H4 Gurupá
53I6 Gurupi
11L9 Gur'yevsk
32D3 Gusau
11M9 Gusev
31A5 Gushan
25L4 Gusinoozersk
22I5 Gus'-Khrustal'nyy
13N4 Güstrow
13L5 Gütersloh
27I4 Guwahati
53G2 Guyana
46G4 Guymon
42E3 Guyra
26F3 Guzar
11L9 Gvardeysk
27G4 Gwalior
35C6 Gwanda
34F2 Gwardafuy, Gees *c.*
35C5 Gweru
35C6 Gweta
32E3 Gwoza
24I2 Gydan Peninsula
41K5 Gympie
13Q7 Gyöngyös
20G1 Győr
21J6 Gytheio
21I1 Gyula
23I8 Gyumri
26E3 Gyzylarbat

H
11M7 Haapsalu
12J4 Haarlem
34E2 Habbān
30F4 Hachinohe
48D2 Hackensack
16G5 Haddington
32E3 Hadejia
11F9 Haderslev
23G6 Hadyach
31B5 Haeju
31B6 Haenam
29G6 Hagåtña
13K5 Hagen
48C3 Hagerstown
11H6 Hagfors
31C6 Hagi
18H2 Haguenau
33G1 Haifa
27K4 Haikou
26D4 Ḥā'il
27K2 Hailar
30C3 Hailin
15H8 Hailsham
30B3 Hailun
27K5 Hainan *i.*
28C5 Hai Phong
51J5 Haiti
21I1 Hajdúböszörmény
34E2 Ḥajjah
30F4 Hakodate
31E5 Hakui
33G2 Halaib Triangle *terr.*
13M5 Halberstadt
11G7 Halden
13M4 Haldensleben
15E6 Halesowen
15I6 Halesworth
14F5 Halifax
45L5 Halifax
11I7 Hällefors
13N7 Hallein
13M5 Halle (Saale)
11I7 Hallsberg
40F3 Halls Creek
29E7 Halmahera *i.*
11H8 Halmstad
11G8 Hals
14E4 Haltwhistle
31D6 Hamada
33H1 Hamadān
33G1 Ḥamāh
31E6 Hamamatsu
11G6 Hamar
27H6 Hambantota
13L4 Hamburg
48B1 Hamburg
48E2 Hamden
11N6 Hämeenlinna
13L4 Hameln
40D4 Hamersley Range *mts*
31B5 Hamhŭng
27I2 Hami
16E5 Hamilton
43E3 Hamilton
47K4 Hamilton
48B1 Hamilton
51L2 Hamilton
11O6 Hamina
31B5 Hamju
13K5 Hamm
32C2 Hammada du Drâa *plat.*
20D6 Hammamet
20D6 Hammamet, Golfe de *g.*
10M1 Hammerfest
48D3 Hammonton
15F7 Hampshire Downs *hills*
48C4 Hampton
34D1 Ḥanak
31F5 Hanamaki
27K3 Handan
35D4 Handeni
49C2 Hanford
27I2 Hangayn Nuruu *mts*
28E4 Hangzhou
28E4 Hangzhou Wan *b.*
11M7 Hanko
44G4 Hanna
47I4 Hannibal
13L4 Hannover
11I9 Hanöbukten *b.*
28C5 Ha Nôi
48C3 Hanover
11O10 Hantsavichy
27J3 Hanzhong
10N4 Haparanda
45L4 Happy Valley - Goose Bay
34E1 Ḥaraḍh
23F5 Haradok
31F5 Haramachi
35D5 Harare
30B3 Harbin
11D7 Hardangerfjorden *sea chan.*
36C3 Hardap *admin. reg.*
34E3 Hārer
34E3 Hargeysa
31D6 Harima-nada *b.*
11M6 Harjavalta
15I6 Harleston
15H7 Harlow
46C3 Harney Basin
10J5 Härnösand
32C4 Harper
16B3 Harris, Sound of *sea chan.*
48C2 Harrisburg
47I4 Harrison
48B3 Harrisonburg
47I4 Harrisonville
14F5 Harrogate
21L2 Hârșova
10J2 Harstad
13O7 Hartberg
48E2 Hartford
14F4 Hartlepool
46G2 Harvey
15I7 Harwich
15G7 Haslemere
27G5 Hassan
12J5 Hasselt
11H8 Hässleholm
15H8 Hastings
43F4 Hastings
46H3 Hastings
47I3 Hastings
14G5 Hatfield
47L4 Hatteras, Cape
47J5 Hattiesburg
29C7 Hat Yai
34E3 Haud *reg.*
11D7 Haugesund
10P5 Haukivesi *l.*
43E3 Hauraki Gulf
32C1 Haut Atlas *mts*
15I9 Haute-Normandie *admin. reg.*
32C1 Hauts Plateaux
51H4 Havana
15G8 Havant
15C7 Haverfordwest
48F1 Haverhill
13O6 Havlíčkův Brod
21L5 Havran
46F2 Havre
39I5 Havre Rock *i.*
23G8 Havza
46□ Hawaii *i.*
16G5 Hawick
43F4 Hawke Bay
14F4 Haxby
42B5 Hay
41H4 Hay *watercourse*
26E5 Haymā'
21L4 Hayrabolu
44G3 Hay River
46H4 Hays
23F6 Haysyn
49A2 Hayward
15G8 Haywards Heath
48D2 Hazleton
15F5 Heanor
7 Heard and McDonald Islands *terr.*
45J5 Hearst
42B6 Heathcote
27J4 Hechi
11I6 Hedemora
27K3 Hefei
30C3 Hegang
13L3 Heide
13L6 Heidelberg
37I4 Heidelberg
30B2 Heihe
13L6 Heilbronn
30C3 Heilongjiang *prov.*
30D2 Heilong Jiang *r.*
11O6 Heinola
10□1 Hekla *vol.*
46E2 Helena
16E4 Helensburgh
13L3 Helgoländer Bucht *g.*
19F4 Hellín
26F3 Helmand *r.*
13J5 Helmond
13M4 Helmstedt
30C4 Helong
11H8 Helsingborg
11H8 Helsingør
11N6 Helsinki
15G7 Hemel Hempstead
49D4 Hemet
21N4 Hendek
47I5 Henderson
47L4 Henderson
49E2 Henderson
13K4 Hengelo
30C3 Hengshan
27K4 Hengyang
23G7 Heniches'k
15G7 Henley-on-Thames
27I5 Henzada
26F3 Herāt
15E6 Hereford
46G5 Hereford
13L4 Herford
18I3 Herisau
48D1 Herkimer
37I6 Hermes, Cape
46E6 Hermosillo
54F3 Hernandarias
15I7 Herne Bay
11F8 Herning
15G9 Hérouville-St-Clair
19D4 Herrera del Duque
48C2 Hershey
15G7 Hertford
49D3 Hesperia
13M5 Hettstedt
14E4 Hexham
14E4 Heysham
14E5 Heywood
27K3 Heze
47I2 Hibbing
46F6 Hidalgo del Parral
55A2 Hidrolândia
48E2 Highlands
48C4 Highland Springs
44G4 High Level
47L4 High Point
44G4 High Prairie
15G7 High Wycombe
51K5 Higüey
11M7 Hiiumaa *i.*
34D1 Hijaz *reg.*
31E6 Hikone
13L4 Hildesheim
33H1 Hillah
11H9 Hillerød
42B4 Hillston
46□ Hilo
47K5 Hilton Head Island
12J4 Hilversum
27G3 Himalaya *mts*
21H4 Himarë
31D6 Himeji
15F6 Hinckley
14E5 Hindley
26F3 Hindu Kush *mts*
47K5 Hinesville
30F4 Hirosaki
31D6 Hiroshima
18G2 Hirson
11F8 Hirtshals
27G4 Hisar
51J4 Hispaniola *i.*
31F5 Hitachi
31F5 Hitachinaka
11I7 Hjälmaren *l.*
11I7 Hjo
11G8 Hjørring
37I5 Hlotse
23G6 Hlukhiv
11O9 Hlybokaye
32D4 Ho
41J8 Hobart
46G5 Hobbs
11F8 Hobro
29C6 Ho Chi Minh City
15G7 Hoddesdon
34E2 Hodeidah
21I1 Hódmezővásárhely
30C4 Hoeryŏng
13M5 Hof
11J6 Hofors
10□1 Hofsjökull *ice cap*
31C6 Hōfu
11H8 Höganäs
32D2 Hoggar *plat.*
27K2 Hohhot
27H3 Hoh Xil Shan *mts*
34D3 Hoima
30F4 Hokkaidō *i.*
11F7 Hokksund
11G9 Holbæk
42C5 Holbrook
46H3 Holdrege
51I4 Holguín
48B2 Hollidaysburg
49B2 Hollister
47J5 Holly Springs
47K6 Hollywood
11G7 Holmestrand
10L5 Holmsund
11F8 Holstebro
15I6 Holt
14C5 Holyhead
14C5 Holyhead Bay
14C5 Holy Island
14F3 Holy Island
32C3 Hombori
45L3 Home Bay
48C1 Homer
33G1 Homs
23F5 Homyel'
21M6 Honaz
46H6 Hondo
51G6 Honduras
11G6 Hønefoss
27J4 Hongjiang
27K4 Hong Kong
31B4 Hongwŏn
28D4 Hongze Hu *l.*
41L1 Honiara
15D8 Honiton
31F5 Honjō
46□ Honolulu
31D6 Honshū *i.*
13K4 Hoogeveen
37G4 Hoopstad
11H9 Höör
12J4 Hoorn
49E2 Hoover Dam
23I8 Hopa
47I5 Hope
48C4 Hopewell
47J4 Hopkinsville
11H9 Hörby
23F5 Horki
23H6 Horlivka
26E4 Hormuz, Strait of
13O6 Horn
54C9 Horn, Cape
14G5 Horncastle
10K5 Hörnefors
42E4 Hornsby
23E6 Horodenka
23F6 Horodnya
23D6 Horodok
23E6 Horodok
11F9 Horsens
15G7 Horsham
41I7 Horsham
11G7 Horten
27G3 Hoshiarpur
27H3 Hotan
47I5 Hot Springs
47J2 Houghton
14F4 Houghton le Spring
47I6 Houma
47H6 Houston
27I2 Hovd
15G8 Hove
11I8 Hovmantorp
27J1 Hövsgöl Nuur *l.*
14G5 Howden
42D6 Howe, Cape
37J5 Howick
39I1 Howland Island *terr.*
42C5 Howlong
13L5 Höxter
16F2 Hoy *i.*
13O5 Hoyerswerda
13O5 Hradec Králové
23J8 Hrazdan
23G6 Hrebinka
11M10 Hrodna
28E5 Hsinchu
52C6 Huacho
30B4 Huadian
27K3 Huaibei
27J4 Huaihua
27K3 Huainan
50E5 Huajuápan de León
35B5 Huambo
30C3 Huanan
52C6 Huancavelica
52C6 Huancayo
30B4 Huanren
52C5 Huánuco
52C5 Huaráz
52C6 Huarmey
54B3 Huasco
46F6 Huatabampo
27G5 Hubli
15F5 Hucknall
14F5 Huddersfield
30A2 Huder
11J6 Hudiksvall
48E1 Hudson
48F1 Hudson
48E2 Hudson *r.*
45J4 Hudson Bay *sea*
48E1 Hudson Falls
45K3 Hudson Strait
29C6 Huê
50F5 Huehuetenango
19C5 Huelva
19F2 Huesca
41I4 Hughenden
49B2 Hughson
47H5 Hugo
36G4 Huhudi
36C4 Huib-Hoch Plateau
35B5 Huíla Plateau
50F5 Huimanguillo
11M6 Huittinen
30B3 Hulan
30A3 Hulan Ergi
34E1 Ḥulayfah
30D3 Hulin
45K5 Hull
11I8 Hultsfred
33G2 Ḥulwān
52F5 Humaitá
14H5 Humber, Mouth of the
42C5 Hume Reservoir
33E2 Hūn
10□1 Húnaflói *b.*
21J2 Hunedoara
20H1 Hungary
31B5 Hŭngnam
15H6 Hunstanton
15G6 Huntingdon
48C2 Huntingdon
47J3 Huntington
47K4 Huntington
49C4 Huntington Beach
16G3 Huntly
45K5 Huntsville
47H5 Huntsville
47J5 Huntsville
46H3 Huron
48A1 Huron, Lake
10□1 Húsavík
21M1 Huși
11D7 Husnes
10K5 Husum
13L3 Husum
46H4 Hutchinson
28E4 Huzhou
20G3 Hvar *i.*
35C5 Hwange
26F4 Hyderabad
27G5 Hyderabad
18H5 Hyères
30C4 Hyesan
15I7 Hythe
31C6 Hyūga
11N6 Hyvinkää

I
55C1 Iaçu
21L2 Ianca
21L1 Iași
32D4 Ibadan
52C3 Ibagué
55A3 Ibaiti
52C3 Ibarra
34E2 Ibb
19 Iberian Peninsula
55B2 Ibiá
53J4 Ibiapaba, Serra da *hills*
55C1 Ibiassucê
55D1 Ibicaraí
55A4 Ibirama
55A3 Ibitinga
19G4 Ibiza
19G4 Ibiza *i.*
53J6 Ibotirama
26E4 Ibrā'
26E4 Ibrī
52C6 Ica
53J4 Icatu
33G1 İçel
10□1 Iceland
31E6 Ichinomiya
31F5 Ichinoseki
23G6 Ichnya
53K5 Icó
55C3 Iconha
32D4 Idah
46E3 Idaho *state*
46E3 Idaho Falls
13K6 Idar-Oberstein
33G2 Idfū
35B4 Idiofa
33G1 Idlib
55A3 Iepê
35D4 Ifakara
35E6 Ifanadiana
32D4 Ife
33E3 Ifenat
32D3 Iferouâne
32D3 Ifôghas, Adrar des *hills*
33G4 Iganga
55B3 Igarapava
24J3 Igarka
11J6 Iggesund
20C5 Iglesias
11O9 Ignalina
21I5 Igoumenitsa
55C1 Iguaí
50E5 Iguala
19G3 Igualada
55B4 Iguape
54F2 Iguatemi
53K5 Iguatu
35E6 Ihosy
10O5 Iisalmi
31C6 Iizuka
32D4 Ijebu-Ode
23J8 Ijevan
13J4 IJssel *r.*
37H4 Ikageng
32D4 Ikare
21L6 Ikaria *i.*
11F8 Ikast
21J3 Ikhtiman
32D4 Ikom
31B6 Iksan
35D4 Ikungu
29E6 Ilagan
33H1 Īlām
13Q4 Iława
35C4 Ilebo
22I3 Ileza
13M5 Ilfeld
15H7 Ilford
15C7 Ilfracombe
23G8 Ilgaz
54F2 Ilha Grande, Represa *resr*
19B3 Ílhavo
55D1 Ilhéus
15F6 Ilkeston
14F5 Ilkley
54B4 Illapel
32D3 Illéla
13L6 Iller *r.*
21N1 Illichivs'k
47I4 Illinois *r.*
47J4 Illinois *state*
32D2 Illizi
22F4 Il'men', Ozero *l.*
15E8 Ilminster
52D7 Ilo
29E6 Iloilo
32D4 Ilorin
23I6 Ilovlya
45M3 Ilulissat
31D6 Imabari
31E5 Imaichi
31C6 Imari
55A5 Imaruí
11P6 Imatra
55A4 Imbituva
20D2 Imola
53I5 Imperatriz
20C3 Imperia
49E4 Imperial
49D4 Imperial Beach
34B3 Impfondo
27I4 Imphal
21K4 İmroz
31E6 Ina
10O2 Inarijärvi *l.*
19H4 Inca
31B5 Inch'ŏn
16C5 Indaal, Loch *b.*
10J5 Indalsälven *r.*
34D2 Inda Silasē
47I4 Independence
30A3 Inder
26E2 Inderborskiy
27G4 India
48B2 Indiana
47J3 Indiana *state*
47J4 Indianapolis
47I3 Indianola
47I5 Indianola
25P2 Indigirka *r.*
21I2 Inđija
49D4 Indio
29D8 Indonesia
27G4 Indore
27F4 Indus *r.*
26F4 Indus, Mouths of the
23G8 İnebolu
21M4 İnegöl
42E2 Inglewood
49C4 Inglewood
14H5 Ingoldmells
13M6 Ingolstadt
37L2 Inhambane
37L2 Inhambane *prov.*
55A2 Inhumas
16D3 Inner Sound *sea chan.*
41J3 Innisfail
13M7 Innsbruck
34B4 Inongo
13Q4 Inowrocław
32D2 In Salah
40C5 Inscription, Cape
24H3 Inta
47I2 International Falls
44E3 Inuvik
43B8 Invercargill
16E3 Invergordon
16F4 Inverkeithing
16E3 Inverness
40G6 Investigator Group *is*
41H7 Investigator Strait
35D4 Inyonga
23J5 Inza
23I5 Inzhavino
21I5 Ioannina
47H4 Iola
16C4 Iona *i.*
21H5 Ionian Islands
20H5 Ionian Sea
21K6 Ios *i.*
47I3 Iowa *state*
47I3 Iowa City
55A2 Ipameri
55C2 Ipanema
55C2 Ipatinga
23I7 Ipatovo
37G4 Ipelegeng
52C3 Ipiales
55D1 Ipiaú
55D1 Ipirá
55A4 Ipiranga
29C7 Ipoh
55A2 Iporá
34C3 Ippy
21L4 İpsala
15I6 Ipswich
42F1 Ipswich
53J4 Ipu
45L3 Iqaluit
54B2 Iquique
52D4 Iquitos
54F3 Irai
21K7 Iraklion
55C1 Iramaia
26E3 Iran
26F4 Īrānshahr
50D4 Irapuato
33H1 Iraq
55D1 Irara
55A4 Irati
33G1 Irbid
24H4 Irbit
53J6 Irecê
17 Ireland *i.*
17E4 Ireland, Republic of
26F2 Irgiz
35D4 Iringa
53H4 Iriri *r.*
17G4 Irish Sea
53I4 Irituia
25L4 Irkutsk
48C1 Irondequoit
47J2 Iron Mountain
29E6 Irosin
23F6 Irpin'
27I5 Irrawaddy *r.*
27G1 Irtysh *r.*
19F2 Irún
16E5 Irvine
49D4 Irvine
32D3 Isa
29E7 Isabela
10□1 Ísafjarðardjúp *est.*
10□1 Ísafjörður
31E6 Ise
18G4 Isère *r.*
20F4 Isernia
31E6 Ise-wan *b.*
32D4 Iseyin
31F5 Ishinomaki
31F5 Ishioka
24I4 Isil'kul'
37J5 Isipingo
34C3 Isiro
33G1 İskenderun
24J4 Iskitim
27G3 Islamabad
43E2 Islands, Bay of
16C5 Islay *i.*
35D5 Isoka
21N6 Isparta
21L3 Isperikh
33G1 Israel
32C4 Issia
18F4 Issoire
21M4 İstanbul
21J5 Istiaia
18G5 Istres
20E2 Istria *pen.*
55A3 Itaberá
55C1 Itaberaba
55A2 Itaberaí
55C2 Itabira
55C3 Itabirito
55D1 Itabuna
53I5 Itacajá
55B1 Itacarambi
53G4 Itacoatiara
55C1 Itaetê
55C2 Itaguaçu
55A3 Itaí
55A4 Itaiópolis
53G4 Itaituba
55A4 Itajaí
55B3 Itajubá
55D1 Itajuípe
20E3 Italy
55C2 Itamarandiba
55C1 Itambé
55B4 Itanhaém
55C2 Itanhém
55C2 Itaobím
55A1 Itapaci
55A2 Itapajipe
55D1 Itapebi
55B3 Itapecerica
55C3 Itapemirim
55C3 Itaperuna
55C1 Itapetinga
55A3 Itapetininga
55A3 Itapeva
53J6 Itapicuru
53J4 Itapicuru Mirim
53K4 Itapipoca
55B3 Itapira
55A3 Itaporanga
55A5 Itapuã
54E3 Itaqui
55A4 Itararé
55B3 Itatiba
55B3 Itaúna
21J5 Itea
48C1 Ithaca
55C2 Itinga
53H7 Itiquira
55C1 Itiruçu
31E6 Itō
55B3 Itu
55C1 Ituaçu
55D1 Ituberá
55A2 Ituiutaba
55A2 Itumbiara
53I5 Itupiranga
55A4 Ituporanga
55A2 Iturama
13L4 Itzehoe
25T3 Iul'tin
10O2 Ivalo
11N10 Ivanava
23F6 Ivankiv
23E6 Ivano-Frankivs'k
30B2 Ivanovka
22I4 Ivanovo
23K5 Ivanteyevka
11N10 Ivatsevichy
21L4 Ivaylovgrad
24H3 Ivdel'
20B2 Ivrea
21L5 İvrindi
45K3 Ivujivik
11O10 Ivyanyets
31F5 Iwaki
31D6 Iwakuni
30F4 Iwamizawa
32D4 Iwo
11N10 Iwye
50E4 Ixmiquilpán
50D4 Ixtlán
15H6 Ixworth
23J8 Izberbash
24G4 Izhevsk
21M2 Izmayil
21L5 İzmir
21L5 İzmir Körfezi *g.*
21K4 Iztochni Rodopi *mts*
31D6 Izumo
23E6 Izyaslav
22M2 Iz''yayu
23H6 Izyum

J
27G4 Jabalpur
20G3 Jablanica
53L5 Jaboatão
55A3 Jaboticabal
55C1 Jacaraci
55B3 Jacareí
55A3 Jacarézinho
55C2 Jacinto
47I5 Jackson
47J4 Jackson
47K3 Jackson
47I4 Jacksonville
47K5 Jacksonville
47L5 Jacksonville
51J5 Jacmel
26F4 Jacobabad
53J6 Jacobina
53I4 Jacunda
19E5 Jaén
41H7 Jaffa, Cape
27G6 Jaffna
27H5 Jagdalpur
55A4 Jaguariaíva
55D1 Jaguaripe
26E4 Jahrom
53J5 Jaicós
27G4 Jaipur
27G4 Jaisalmer
29C8 Jakarta
10M5 Jakobstad
27G3 Jalālābād
27G3 Jalandhar
50E5 Jalapa
55A3 Jales
27G4 Jalgaon
32E4 Jalingo
27G5 Jalna
50D4 Jalpa
27H4 Jalpaiguri
51I5 Jamaica
51I5 Jamaica Channel
29C8 Jambi
46H3 James *r.*
45J4 James Bay
41H6 Jamestown
46H2 Jamestown
48B1 Jamestown
27G3 Jammu
11N6 Jämsä
10N6 Jämsänkoski
27H4 Jamshedpur
55C1 Janaúba
47J3 Janesville
55B1 Januária
31D5 Japan
31D5 Japan, Sea of
52F4 Japurá *r.*
55A1 Jaraguá
55A4 Jaraguá do Sul
55B3 Jardinópolis
13P5 Jarocin
23D6 Jarosław
48C3 Jarrettsville
52F6 Jarú
11N6 Järvenpää
26E4 Jāsk
23D6 Jasło
44G4 Jasper
47I5 Jasper
13Q6 Jastrzębie-Zdrój
21H1 Jászberény
55A2 Jataí
55A3 Jaú
52C6 Jauja
29C8 Java *i.*
29D8 Jawa, Laut *sea*
34E3 Jawhar
13P5 Jawor
29F8 Jaya, Puncak *mt.*
29G8 Jayapura
16G5 Jedburgh
34D1 Jeddah
47I4 Jefferson City
36G8 Jeffrey's Bay
11N8 Jēkabpils
13O5 Jelenia Góra
11M8 Jelgava
29D8 Jember
13M5 Jena
20C6 Jendouba
47I5 Jennings
55C1 Jequié
55C2 Jequitinhonha
51J5 Jérémie
50D4 Jerez
19C5 Jerez de la Frontera
46E3 Jerome
15E9 Jersey *terr.*
48D2 Jersey City
53J5 Jerumenha
33G1 Jerusalem
42E5 Jervis Bay
42E5 Jervis Bay Territory *admin. div.*
20F1 Jesenice
20E3 Jesi
11G6 Jessheim
47K5 Jesup
27G4 Jhansi
30C3 Jiamusi
27K4 Ji'an
30B4 Ji'an
28D5 Jianyang
30B4 Jiaohe
28E4 Jiaxing
27I3 Jiayuguan
11N9 Jieznas
13O6 Jihlava
32D1 Jijel
34E3 Jijiga
34E3 Jilib
30B4 Jilin
30B4 Jilin *prov.*
34D3 Jīma
46G6 Jiménez
46H7 Jiménez
48D2 Jim Thorpe
27K3 Jinan
13O6 Jindřichův Hradec
28D5 Jingdezhen
42C5 Jingellic
30B4 Jingyu
27J3 Jingyuan
27K3 Jingzhou
28D5 Jinhua
27K2 Jining
27K3 Jining
34D3 Jinja
51G6 Jinotepe
28D5 Jinxi
27K3 Jinzhong
27L2 Jinzhou
52F6 Ji-Paraná
52B4 Jipijapa
55D1 Jiquiricá
27J4 Jishou
30A2 Jiwen
30C3 Jixi
30C3 Jixian
34E2 Jīzān
55A4 Joaçaba
55C2 Joaíma
53L5 João Pessoa
55B2 João Pinheiro
27G4 Jodhpur
10P5 Joensuu
31E5 Jōetsu
11O7 Jõgeva
37H4 Johannesburg
46D3 John Day
16F2 John o'Groats
48B2 Johnsonburg
16E5 Johnstone
48B2 Johnstown
48D1 Johnstown
29C7 Johor Bahru
11O7 Jõhvi
18G2 Joinville
55A4 Joinville
47J3 Joliet
11N9 Jonava
47I4 Jonesboro
45J2 Jones Sound *sea chan.*
11I8 Jönköping
45K5 Jonquière
47I4 Joplin
33G1 Jordan
27I4 Jorhat
32D4 Jos
54B6 José de San Martin
40F2 Joseph Bonaparte Gulf
32D4 Jos Plateau
37H4 Jouberton
11P6 Joutseno
46G7 Juan Aldama
44F5 Juan de Fuca Strait
53J5 Juàzeiro
53K5 Juàzeiro do Norte
33G4 Juba
34E4 Jubba *r.*
19F4 Júcar *r.*
55A1 Juçara
50E5 Juchitán
13O7 Judenburg
51G6 Juigalpa
53G6 Juína
55C3 Juiz de Fora
52D7 Juliaca
19F4 Jumilla
27G4 Junagadh
47H4 Junction City
55B3 Jundiaí
44E4 Juneau
42C5 Junee
18H3 Jungfrau *mt.*
54D4 Junín
11N8 Juodupė
16D4 Jura *i.*
18G4 Jura *mts*
16D5 Jura, Sound of *sea chan.*
11M9 Jurbarkas
11M8 Jūrmala
53G4 Juruti
52E5 Jutaí
50G6 Jutiapa
51G6 Juticalpa
11F8 Jutland *pen.*
36G3 Jwaneng
10N5 Jyväskylä

K
27G3 K2 *mt.*
11M6 Kaarina
34C4 Kabale
35C4 Kabalo
35C4 Kabinda
35C4 Kabongo
27F3 Kābul
35C5 Kabwe
27G4 Kachchh, Rann of *marsh*
32D4 Kachia
23J8 Kachret'i
25L4 Kachug
21M4 Kadıköy
35C5 Kadoma
33F3 Kadugli
32D3 Kaduna
22H4 Kaduy
22L2 Kadzherom
32B3 Kaédi
33E3 Kaélé
31B5 Kaesŏng
32D4 Kafanchan
35C5 Kafue
35C5 Kafue *r.*
31E5 Kaga
34B3 Kaga Bandoro
31C7 Kagoshima
31C7 Kagoshima *pref.*
23F6 Kaharlyk
26C3 Kahramanmaraș
27K3 Kaifeng
31D6 Kainan
20D7 Kairouan
27J4 Kaiyuan
30B4 Kaiyuan
10O4 Kajaani
34D3 Kakamega
32B4 Kakata
21O1 Kakhovka
27H5 Kakinada
31D6 Kakogawa
35D4 Kala
20D7 Kalaâ Kebira
23I6 Kalach
23I6 Kalach-na-Donu
35C6 Kalahari Desert
10M4 Kalajoki
21J4 Kalamaria
21J6 Kalamata
47J3 Kalamazoo
21O1 Kalanchak
21M6 Kale
35C4 Kalemie
10Q4 Kalevala
40E6 Kalgoorlie
20F2 Kali
34C4 Kalima
11L9 Kaliningrad
23J6 Kalininsk
23H7 Kalininskaya
23F5 Kalinkavichy
46E2 Kalispell
13Q5 Kalisz
10M4 Kalix
11J8 Kalmar
23H5 Kaluga
11G9 Kalundborg
23E6 Kalush
22H4 Kalyazin
34C4 Kama
22L4 Kama *r.*
31F5 Kamaishi
35C5 Kambove
25Q4 Kamchatka Peninsula
23J5 Kamenka
23K6 Kamenka
24J4 Kamen'-na-Obi
23I7 Kamenolomni
23I6 Kamensk-Shakhtinskiy
24H4 Kamensk-Ural'skiy
35C4 Kamina
44F4 Kamloops
23J8 Kamo
34D3 Kampala
34C4 Kampene
29C6 Kâmpóng Cham
29C6 Kâmpóng Spœ
29C6 Kâmpóng Thum
29C6 Kâmpôt
34D3 Kamuli
23E6 Kam''yanets'-Podil's'kyy
23E6 Kam''yanka-Buz'ka
11M10 Kamyanyets
33H1 Kāmyārān
23J6 Kamyshin
23K7 Kamyzyak
35C4 Kananga
22J5 Kanash
31E5 Kanazawa
27G5 Kanchipuram
26F3 Kandahār
10R3 Kandalaksha
32D4 Kandé
32D3 Kandi
21N4 Kandıra
42D4 Kandos
27H6 Kandy
26E2 Kandyagash
46□ Kaneohe
23H7 Kanevskaya
26E4 Kangān
29C7 Kangar
41H7 Kangaroo Island
30B4 Kanggye
31C5 Kangnŭng
30A4 Kangping
32B3 Kanifing
22J2 Kanin, Poluostrov *pen.*
11M6 Kankaanpää
47J3 Kankakee
32C3 Kankan
32D3 Kano
31C7 Kanoya
27H4 Kanpur
46H4 Kansas *state*
47I4 Kansas City
25K4 Kansk
32D3 Kantchari
23H6 Kantemirovka
37J3 KaNyamazane
37G3 Kanye
28E5 Kaohsiung
32B3 Kaolack
35C5 Kapiri Mposhi
33G4 Kapoeta
20G1 Kaposvár
45J5 Kapuskasing
20G1 Kapuvár
11O10 Kapyl'
32D4 Kara
26F1 Karabalyk
26E2 Kara-Bogaz-Gol, Zaliv *b.*
23G8 Karabük
21M4 Karacabey
21M6 Karacasu
23I8 Karachayevsk
23G5 Karachev
26F4 Karachi
27G2 Karaganda
27G2 Karagayly
21M5 Karahallı
26E3 Karaj
27G2 Kara-Köl
27G2 Karakol
27G3 Karakoram Range *mts*
26E2 Karakum Desert
26F3 Karakum Desert
33G1 Karaman
21M6 Karamanlı
27H2 Karamay
43C5 Karamea Bight *b.*
21M4 Karamürsel
36C4 Karas *admin. reg.*
36D5 Karasburg
24I2 Kara Sea
21N4 Karasu
24I4 Karasuk
27G2 Karatau
31C6 Karatsu
33H1 Karbalā'
21I1 Karcag
21I5 Karditsa
11M7 Kärdla
33G3 Kareima
10R5 Kareliya, Respublika *aut. rep.*
35D4 Karema
23J8 Kargalinskaya
22H3 Kargopol'
32E3 Kari
35C5 Kariba
35C5 Kariba, Lake *resr*
35C5 Kariba Dam
29C8 Karimata, Selat *strait*
11N7 Karksi-Nuia
23G6 Karlivka
20F2 Karlovac
21K3 Karlovo
13N5 Karlovy Vary
11I8 Karlshamn
11I7 Karlskoga
11I8 Karlskrona
13L6 Karlsruhe
11H7 Karlstad
27G4 Karnal
21L3 Karnobat
35C5 Karoi
35D4 Karonga
21I5 Karpenisi
22J2 Karpogory
40D4 Karratha
23I8 Kars
11O8 Kārsava
26F3 Karshi
23J5 Karsun
21M4 Kartal
24H4 Kartaly
13Q6 Karviná
27G5 Karwar
25M4 Karymskoye
21K5 Karystos
35C4 Kasaï, Plateau du
35D5 Kasama
35C5 Kasane
34D3 Kasese
26E3 Kāshān
23I6 Kashary
27G3 Kashi
31D6 Kashihara
22H4 Kashin
23H5 Kashira
31E5 Kashiwazaki
26E3 Kāshmar
23I5 Kasimov
35C4 Kasongo
35B4 Kasongo-Lunda
23J8 Kaspiysk
33G3 Kassala
13L5 Kassel
20C7 Kasserine
23G8 Kastamonu
21J7 Kastelli
21I4 Kastoria
23G5 Kastsyukovichy
35D4 Kasulu
35D5 Kasungu
34D3 Katakwi
21J4 Katerini
35D5 Katete
37I4 Kathlehong
27H4 Kathmandu
32C3 Kati
27H4 Katihar
35C5 Katima Mulilo
32C4 Katiola
21I5 Kato Achaïa
42E4 Katoomba
13Q5 Katowice
33G2 Kātrīnā, Jabal *mt.*
16E4 Katrine, Loch *l.*
11J7 Katrineholm
32D3 Katsina
32D4 Katsina-Ala
31F6 Katsuura
11G8 Kattegat *strait*
46□ Kauai Channel
10M5 Kauhajoki
10M5 Kauhava
11M9 Kaunas
32D3 Kaura-Namoda
21J4 Kavadarci
23H8 Kavak
21K4 Kavala
30D3 Kavalerovo
21M3 Kavarna
26E3 Kavīr, Dasht-e *des.*
31E6 Kawagoe
31E6 Kawaguchi
31E6 Kawasaki
33G2 Kawm Umbū
32C3 Kaya
32B3 Kayes
26C3 Kayseri
27G1 Kazakhskiy Melkosopochnik *plain*
26F2 Kazakhstan
22K5 Kazan'
21K3 Kazanlŭk
21L5 Kaz Dağı *mts*
23D6 Kazincbarcika
17F3 Keady
46H3 Kearney
32D1 Kebili
21N6 Keçiborlu
21H1 Kecskemét
11M9 Kėdainiai
30B3 Kedong
13Q5 Kędzierzyn-Koźle
48E1 Keene
36D4 Keetmanshoop
32D4 Keffi
10□1 Keflavík
27G2 Kegen
11N7 Kehra
14F5 Keighley
16G3 Keith
41I7 Keith
20D6 Kelibia
26C2 Kelkit *r.*
11M9 Kelmė
33E4 Kelo
44G5 Kelowna
29C7 Keluang
22G2 Kem'
21L5 Kemalpaşa
21N6 Kemer
24J4 Kemerovo
10N4 Kemi
10O3 Kemijärvi
16G3 Kemnay
10N4 Kempele
13M7 Kempten (Allgäu)
37I4 Kempton Park
14E4 Kendal
29E8 Kendari
29D8 Kendawangan
32B4 Kenema
35B4 Kenge
36E5 Kenhardt
32C1 Kénitra
48B1 Kenmore
46D2 Kennewick
47J3 Kenosha
48A2 Kent
47K4 Kentucky *state*
34D3 Kenya
34D4 Kenya, Mount
47I3 Keokuk
41K4 Keppel Bay
21M5 Kepsut
42A5 Kerang
11N6 Kerava
19G5 Kerba
23H7 Kerch
38E2 Kerema
33G3 Keren
32B3 Kerewan
34D4 Kericho
26F3 Kerki
21H5 Kerkyra
39I5 Kermadec Islands
26E3 Kermān
33H1 Kermānshāh
46G5 Kermit
46H5 Kerrville
11G9 Kerteminde
21L4 Keșan
23H8 Keșap
31F5 Kesennuma
30B2 Keshan
10Q4 Kesten'ga
14D4 Keswick
20G1 Keszthely
29D8 Ketapang
15G6 Kettering
10N5 Keuruu
30A2 Keyihe
47K6 Key Largo
15E7 Keynsham
48B3 Keyser
47K7 Key West
36E3 Kgalagadi *admin. dist.*
37H3 Kgatleng *admin. dist.*
37H4 Kgotsong
30D2 Khabarovsk
30D2 Khabarovskiy Kray *admin. div.*
27F4 Khairpur
25L4 Khamar-Daban, Khrebet *mts*
27G4 Khamgaon
34E2 Khamis Mushayṭ
25O3 Khandyga
30D3 Khanka, Lake
27G4 Khanpur
24H3 Khanty-Mansiysk
23J7 Kharabali
27H4 Kharagpur
33G2 Khārijah, Wāḥāt al *oasis*
23H6 Kharkiv
21K4 Kharmanli
22I4 Kharovsk
33G3 Khartoum
23J8 Khasav'yurt
26F4 Khāsh
23I8 Khashuri
21K4 Khaskovo
34D1 Khaybar
36D8 Khayelitsha
19H5 Khemis Miliana
20B7 Khenchela
32C1 Khenifra
21O1 Kherson
25M4 Khilok
23H5 Khlevnoye
23E6 Khmel'nyts'kyy
23E6 Khmil'nyk
26E2 Khodzheyli
36C2 Khomas *admin. reg.*
29C6 Khon Kaen
30D3 Khor
23G6 Khorol
30D3 Khorol
33H1 Khorramābād
33H1 Khorramshahr
27G3 Khorugh
32C1 Khouribga
26E1 Khromtau
23F6 Khrystynivka
27F2 Khŭjand
34D1 Khulays
27H4 Khulna
37H4 Khuma
34E1 Khurayș
23D6 Khust
37H4 Khutsong
23K5 Khvalynsk
22G4 Khvoynaya
27G3 Khyber Pass
42E5 Kiama
35D4 Kibaha
34D3 Kiboga
33G4 Kibre Mengist
34D4 Kibungo
21I4 Kičevo
22J4 Kichmengskiy Gorodok
32D3 Kidal
15E6 Kidderminster
15E5 Kidsgrove
13M3 Kiel
13R5 Kielce
14E3 Kielder Water *resr*
13M3 Kieler Bucht *b.*
23F6 Kiev
32B3 Kiffa
21J5 Kifisia
34D4 Kigali
35C4 Kigoma
21I2 Kikinda
22J4 Kiknur
35B4 Kikwit
30C4 Kilchu
17F4 Kilcoole
42F1 Kilcoy
17F4 Kildare
10R2 Kil'dinstroy
34D4 Kilimanjaro *vol.*
11N7 Kilingi-Nõmme
21M2 Kiliya
17G3 Kilkeel
17E5 Kilkenny
21J4 Kilkis
17C5 Killarney
46H5 Killeen
16E5 Kilmarnock
22K4 Kil'mez'
42B6 Kilmore
35D4 Kilosa
16E5 Kilwinning
38F2 Kimbe
36G5 Kimberley
40F3 Kimberley Plateau
31C4 Kimch'aek
31C5 Kimch'ŏn
31C6 Kimhae
23H5 Kimovsk
35B4 Kimpese
22H4 Kimry
29D7 Kinabalu, Gunung *mt.*
16F4 Kincardine
46F1 Kindersley
32B3 Kindia
34C4 Kindu
23K5 Kinel'
22I4 Kineshma
11P7 Kingisepp
41I7 King Island
40E3 King Leopold Ranges *hills*
49E3 Kingman
15H6 King's Lynn
40E3 King Sound *b.*
47K4 Kingsport
39G4 Kingston
45K5 Kingston
48D2 Kingston
48D2 Kingston
51I5 Kingston
14G5 Kingston upon Hull
51L6 Kingstown
46H6 Kingsville
15D6 Kington
45I3 King William Island
37H7 King William's Town
16F3 Kinloss
11H8 Kinna
16F4 Kinross
35B4 Kinshasa
47L4 Kinston
16G3 Kintore
16D5 Kintyre *pen.*
35C5 Kipushi
39G3 Kirakira
25L4 Kirensk
23H5 Kireyevsk
39J2 Kiribati
26C3 Kırıkkale
22H4 Kirillov
22G4 Kirishi
21L5 Kırkağaç
14E5 Kirkby
15F5 Kirkby in Ashfield
16F4 Kirkcaldy
16E6 Kirkcudbright
10Q2 Kirkenes
16E5 Kirkintilloch
11N6 Kirkkonummi
45J5 Kirkland Lake
21L4 Kırklareli
47I3 Kirksville
33H1 Kirkūk
16G2 Kirkwall
22K4 Kirov
23G5 Kirov
22K4 Kirovo-Chepetsk
23G6 Kirovohrad
10R3 Kirovsk
22F4 Kirovsk
23G7 Kirovs'ke
30D3 Kirovskiy
22L4 Kirs
23I5 Kirsanov
10L3 Kiruna
31E5 Kiryū
34C3 Kisangani
24J4 Kiselevsk
32D4 Kishi
27G1 Kishkenekol'
34D4 Kisii
21H1 Kiskunfélegyháza
21H1 Kiskunhalas
23I8 Kislovodsk
34E4 Kismaayo
33F5 Kisoro
32B4 Kissidougou
47K6 Kissimmee
34D4 Kisumu
32C3 Kita
31F5 Kitaibaraki
31F5 Kitakami
31C6 Kita-Kyūshū
34D3 Kitale
30F4 Kitami
48A1 Kitchener
10Q5 Kitee
34D3 Kitgum
48B2 Kittanning
35C5 Kitwe
10O5 Kiuruvesi
34C4 Kivu, Lake
24G4 Kizel
23J8 Kizil''yurt
23J8 Kizlyar
22K4 Kizner
13O5 Kladno
13O7 Klagenfurt
11L9 Klaipėda
10□2 Klaksvík
44F5 Klamath *r.*
46C3 Klamath Falls
13N6 Klatovy
37H4 Klerksdorp
23G5 Kletnya
23I6 Kletskaya
23G5 Klimovo
22H4 Klin
23G5 Klintsy
20G2 Ključ
13P5 Kłodzko
13P6 Klosterneuburg
13Q5 Kluczbork
11O10 Klyetsk
25R4 Klyuchevskaya, Sopka *vol.*
14F4 Knaresborough
15D6 Knighton
13O7 Knittelfeld
21J3 Knjaževac
17D5 Knockmealdown Mts *hills*
47K4 Knoxville
36F8 Knysna
31D6 Kōbe
13K5 Koblenz
11N10 Kobryn
23I8 K'obulet'i
21M4 Kocaeli
21J4 Kočani
20F2 Kočevje
31D6 Kōchi
23I7 Kochubeyevskoye
44C4 Kodiak
44C4 Kodiak Island
22H3 Kodino
23F6 Kodyma
32C4 Koforidua
31E6 Kōfu
11H9 Køge
11N7 Kohila
27I4 Kohima
11O7 Kohtla-Järve
27G2 Kokand
10M5 Kokkola
47J3 Kokomo
37H4 Kokosi
27H2 Kokpekti
27F1 Kokshetau
37I6 Kokstad
10R2 Kola
29E8 Kolaka
22H2 Kola Peninsula
22H4 Kol'chugino
32B3 Kolda
11F9 Kolding
19H5 Koléa
27G5 Kolhapur
27H4 Kolkata
13O3 Kołobrzeg
32C3 Kolokani
23H5 Kolomna
23E6 Kolomyya
32C3 Kolondiéba
38C2 Kolonedale
24J4 Kolpashevo
33H3 Koluli
35C5 Kolwezi
25R3 Kolyma *r.*
25R3 Kolymskiy, Khrebet *mts*
23J5 Kolyshley
31E6 Komaki
13Q7 Komárno
31E5 Komatsu
21N1 Kominternivs'ke
20G3 Komiža
20H1 Komló
21K4 Komotini
23G6 Komsomol's'k
30E2 Komsomol'sk-na-Amure
35D4 Kondoa
22G3 Kondopoga
23G5 Kondrovo
45P2 Kong Christian X Land *reg.*
45M3 Kong Frederik IX Land *reg.*
35C4 Kongolo
32C3 Kongoussi
11F7 Kongsberg
11H6 Kongsvinger
13Q4 Konin
22I3 Konosha
23G6 Konotop
30B2 Konstantinovka
13L7 Konstanz
33G1 Konya
20E2 Koper
11J7 Köping
20G1 Koprivnica
23I5 Korablino
21I4 Korçë
20G3 Korčula
20G3 Korčula *i.*
31B5 Korea, North
31B5 Korea, South
31B5 Korea Bay *g.*
31C6 Korea Strait
23H7 Korenovsk
23E6 Korets'
21M4 Körfez
32C4 Korhogo
31F5 Kōriyama
21N6 Korkuteli
27H2 Korla
20G1 Körmend
32C3 Koro
39H3 Koro *i.*
21O4 Köroğlu Dağları *mts*
35D4 Korogwe
29F7 Koror
23F6 Korosten'
23F6 Korostyshiv
30F3 Korsakov
11G9 Korsør
23F6 Korsun'-Shevchenkivs'kyy
12I5 Kortrijk
22J3 Koryazhma
31C6 Koryŏng
21L6 Kos *i.*
31B5 Kosan
13P4 Kościan
42D6 Kosciuszko, Mount
23K5 Koshki
23D6 Košice
31C5 Kosŏng
21I3 Kosovo *prov.*
21I3 Kosovska Mitrovica
26F1 Kostanay
21J3 Kostenets
21J3 Kostinbrod
10Q4 Kostomuksha
23E6 Kostopil'
22I4 Kostroma
23H6 Kostyantynivka
13P3 Koszalin
20G1 Kőszeg
27G4 Kota
29D8 Kotabaru
29C7 Kota Bharu
29D7 Kota Kinabalu
22K4 Kotel'nich
23I7 Kotel'nikovo

35D4 Mohoro
23E6 Mohyliv Podil's'kyy
21L1 Moinești
10I3 Mo i Rana
49D3 Mojave Desert
55B3 Moji das Cruzes
37I5 Mokhotlong
20D7 Moknine
33E3 Mokolo
31B6 Mokp'o
23J6 Mokrous
23J5 Mokshan
10E5 Molde
23F7 Moldova
21M1 Moldovei de Sud, Cîmpia *plain*
37G3 Molepolole
11N9 Molėtai
20G4 Molfetta
19F3 Molina de Aragón
52D7 Mollendo
11H8 Mölnlycke
42D4 Molong
36E5 Molopo *watercourse*
33E4 Moloundou
29E8 Moluccas *is*
53K5 Mombaça
34D4 Mombasa
21K4 Momchilgrad
52D2 Mompós
11H9 Møn *i.*
18H5 Monaco
16E3 Monadhliath Mountains
17F3 Monaghan
20D7 Monastir
23F6 Monastyryshche
30F3 Monbetsu
20B2 Moncalieri
10R3 Monchegorsk
13K5 Mönchengladbach
46G6 Monclova
45L5 Moncton
37J4 Mondlo
20B2 Mondovì
20E4 Mondragone
20E2 Monfalcone
19C2 Monforte
34D3 Mongbwalu
27J4 Mông Cai
33E3 Mongo
27J2 Mongolia
35C5 Mongu
35D5 Monkey Bay
15E7 Monmouth
20G4 Monopoli
19F3 Monreal del Campo
20E5 Monreale
47I5 Monroe
32B4 Monrovia
12I5 Mons
21J3 Montana
46F2 Montana *state*
18F3 Montargis
18E4 Montauban
18G4 Montbrison
18G3 Montceau-les-Mines
18D5 Mont-de-Marsan
53H4 Monte Alegre
55B1 Monte Alegre de Goiás
55A2 Monte Alegre de Minas
55C1 Monte Azul
55A3 Monte Azul Paulista
20E2 Montebelluna
18H5 Monte-Carlo
51J5 Monte Cristi
51I5 Montego Bay
18G4 Montélimar
46H6 Montemorelos
19B4 Montemor-o-Novo
49B2 Monterey
49A2 Monterey Bay
52C2 Montería
54C3 Monteros
46G6 Monterrey
53K6 Monte Santo
55C2 Montes Claros
20F3 Montesilvano
20D3 Montevarchi
54E4 Montevideo
47J5 Montgomery
48A3 Montgomery
18H3 Monthey
48D2 Monticello
19D5 Montilla
18F3 Montluçon
45K5 Montmagny
41K4 Monto
47M3 Montpelier
18F5 Montpellier
45K5 Montréal
16G4 Montrose
46F4 Montrose
51L5 Montserrat *terr.*
15I9 Mont-St-Aignan
27I4 Monywa
20C2 Monza
40D6 Moora
47H2 Moorhead
42B6 Mooroopna
44H4 Moose Jaw
35C6 Mopipi
32C3 Mopti
52D7 Moquegua
11I6 Mora
33E3 Mora
53K5 Morada Nova
35E5 Moramanga
16D4 Morar, Loch *l.*
16E3 Moray Firth *b.*
23I5 Mordovo
14E4 Morecambe
14D4 Morecambe Bay
42D2 Moree
50D5 Morelia
19F3 Morella
19C5 Morena, Sierra *mts*
21K2 Moreni
49D4 Moreno Valley
49B2 Morgan Hill
47K4 Morganton
48B3 Morgantown
18H3 Morges
31F5 Morioka
42E4 Morisset
22K4 Morki
18C2 Morlaix
14F5 Morley
41H3 Mornington Island
32C1 Morocco
35D4 Morogoro
29E7 Moro Gulf
35E6 Morombe
27J2 Mörön
35E6 Morondava
19D5 Morón de la Frontera
35E5 Moroni
34D3 Moroto
23I6 Morozovsk
14F3 Morpeth
55A2 Morrinhos
47K4 Morristown
48D2 Morristown
48D1 Morrisville
53J6 Morro do Chapéu
23I5 Morshanka
20C7 Morsott
54D4 Morteros
42A7 Mortlake
42E5 Moruya
16D4 Morvern *reg.*
42C7 Morwell
13L6 Mosbach
22H5 Moscow
46D2 Moscow
18H2 Moselle *r.*
46D2 Moses Lake
34D4 Moshi
10H4 Mosjøen
13P7 Mosonmagyaróvár
11G7 Moss
36F8 Mossel Bay
41J3 Mossman
53K5 Mossoró
13N5 Most
19G6 Mostaganem
20G3 Mostar
23I7 Mostovskoy
33H1 Mosul
11I7 Motala
16F5 Motherwell
19F4 Motilla del Palancar
19E5 Motril
21J2 Motru
50G4 Motul
34B4 Mouila
18F3 Moulins
27I5 Moulmein
47K5 Moultrie
33E4 Moundou
48A3 Moundsville
46D3 Mountain Home
47I4 Mountain Home
35D5 Mount Darwin
41I7 Mount Gambier
38E2 Mount Hagen
48D3 Mount Holly
41H4 Mount Isa
40D5 Mount Magnet
17E4 Mountmellick
48C1 Mount Morris
47I3 Mount Pleasant
47I5 Mount Pleasant
47K3 Mount Pleasant
15B8 Mount's Bay
46C3 Mount Shasta
46C2 Mount Vernon
47J4 Mount Vernon
19C4 Moura
41J4 Moura
33F3 Mourdi, Dépression du *depr.*
32C3 Mourdiah
17F3 Mourne Mountains *hills*
12I5 Mouscron
32D2 Mouydir, Monts du *plat.*
37H6 Moyeni
52C5 Moyobamba
35D6 Mozambique
35E6 Mozambique Channel
23J8 Mozdok
23H5 Mozhaysk
22L4 Mozhga
35D4 Mpanda
35D5 Mpika
37I4 Mpumalanga *prov.*
35D4 Mpwapwa
20D7 M'Saken
19I6 M'Sila
23F5 Mstsislaw
23H5 Mtsensk
35E5 Mtwara
29C6 Muang Khammouan
34D3 Mubende
32E3 Mubi
35C5 Muconda
55D2 Mucuri
30C3 Mudanjiang
21M4 Mudanya
21N4 Mudurnu
35C5 Mufulira
21M6 Muğla
13M5 Mühlhausen (Thüringen)
29C7 Mui Ca Mau *c.*
17F5 Muine Bheag
16E3 Muir of Ord
31B5 Muju
23D6 Mukacheve
34E2 Mukalla
30C3 Mulan
19E5 Mulhacén *mt.*
18H3 Mulhouse
30C3 Muling
16D4 Mull *i.*
16C4 Mull, Sound of *sea chan.*
48A4 Mullens
17E4 Mullingar
16D5 Mull of Kintyre *hd*
42F2 Mullumbimby
27G3 Multan
27G5 Mumbai
50G4 Muna
15I6 Mundesley
41K5 Mundubbera
27H4 Munger
13M6 Munich
13K5 Münster
13M4 Münster
55C3 Muqui
31E5 Murakami
34C4 Muramvya
22K4 Murashi
21L4 Muratlı
19F5 Murcia
19F5 Murcia *reg.*
21I1 Mureșul *r.*
18E5 Muret
47J4 Murfreesboro
55C3 Muriaé
13N4 Müritz *l.*
10R2 Murmansk
10S2 Murmanskaya Oblast' *admin. div.*
22I5 Murom
30F4 Muroran
31D6 Muroto
47J4 Murray
42A5 Murray *r.*
41H7 Murray Bridge
42A5 Murrumbidgee *r.*
42D5 Murrumburrah
20G1 Murska Sobota
27H4 Murwara
33E2 Murzūq
13O7 Mürzzuschlag
21J3 Musala *mt.*
30C4 Musan
26E4 Muscat
47I3 Muscatine
40G5 Musgrave Ranges *mts*
34B4 Mushie
47H4 Muskogee
34D4 Musoma
16F5 Musselburgh
21M4 Mustafakemalpaşa
42E4 Muswellbrook
33F2 Mūţ
35D5 Mutare
35D5 Mutoko
35E5 Mutsamudu
30F4 Mutsu
55C2 Mutum
34D4 Muyinga
27H4 Muzaffarpur
46G6 Múzquiz
35D5 Mvuma
34D4 Mwanza
35C4 Mwene-Ditu
35C4 Mweru, Lake
11O9 Myadzyel
27I4 Myanmar
27I4 Myingyan
27I4 Myitkyina
21O1 Mykolayiv
21K6 Mykonos *i.*
27I4 Mymensingh
30C4 Myŏnggan
11O9 Myory
10□1 Mýrdalsjökull *ice cap*
23G6 Myrhorod
23F6 Myronivka
47L5 Myrtle Beach
42C6 Myrtleford
13O4 Myślibórz
27G5 Mysore
29C6 My Tho
21L5 Mytilini
21L5 Mytilini Strait
22H5 Mytishchi
35D5 Mzimba
35D5 Mzuzu

N

11M6 Naantali
17F4 Naas
31E6 Nabari
35D4 Naberera
24G4 Naberezhnyye Chelny
20D6 Nabeul
35E5 Nacala
35D5 Nachingwea
47I5 Nacogdoches
19E6 Nador
23E6 Nadvirna
24I3 Nadym
11G9 Næstved
21J6 Nafplio
23J8 Naftalan
34E1 Nafy
29E6 Naga
42B6 Nagambie
31E5 Nagano
31E5 Nagaoka
31C6 Nagasaki
31C6 Nagato
27G6 Nagercoil
31E6 Nagoya
27G4 Nagpur
27I3 Nagqu
20G1 Nagyatád
20G1 Nagykanizsa
33H1 Nahāvand
16F3 Nairn
34D4 Nairobi
30A2 Naji
30C4 Najin
34E2 Najrān
33G4 Nakasongola
31C6 Nakatsu
31E6 Nakatsugawa
33G3 Nakfa
30D4 Nakhodka
29C6 Nakhon Pathom
29C6 Nakhon Ratchasima
29C6 Nakhon Sawan
29B7 Nakhon Si Thammarat
11G9 Nakskov
34D4 Nakuru
23I8 Nal'chik
21N4 Nallıhan
32E1 Nālūt
37I4 Namahadi
27G2 Namangan
42F1 Nambour
42F3 Nambucca Heads
29C5 Nam Đinh
36B3 Namib Desert
35B5 Namibe
35B6 Namibia
46D3 Nampa
32C3 Nampala
31B5 Namp'o
35D5 Nampula
10G4 Namsos
25N3 Namtsy
27I4 Namtu
12J5 Namur
31B6 Namwŏn
29C6 Nan
44F5 Nanaimo
31E5 Nanao
30C3 Nancha
27K4 Nanchang
27J3 Nanchong
18H2 Nancy
27G5 Nanded
32E4 Nanga Eboko
35D4 Nangulangwa
28D4 Nanjing
27K4 Nan Ling *mts*
27J4 Nanning
45N3 Nanortalik
28D5 Nanping
18D3 Nantes
48A1 Nanticoke
48D2 Nanticoke
48F2 Nantucket Sound *g.*
15E5 Nantwich
55C2 Nanuque
27K3 Nanyang
34D4 Nanyuki
49A1 Napa
43F4 Napier
20F4 Naples
47K6 Naples
31D6 Nara
32C3 Nara
11O9 Narach
41I7 Naracoorte
52C4 Naranjal
18F5 Narbonne
20H4 Nardò
45K2 Nares Strait
23J7 Narimanov
27G4 Narmada *r.*
20E3 Narni
24G3 Narodnaya, Gora *mt.*
23H5 Naro-Fominsk
42E6 Narooma
23F6 Narowlya
10L5 Närpes
42C5 Narrandera
42D4 Narromine
45N3 Narsaq
23I8 Nartkala
31D6 Naruto
11P7 Narva
11O7 Narva Bay
10J2 Narvik
22L2 Nar'yan-Mar
27G2 Naryn
27G4 Nashik
48F1 Nashua
47J4 Nashville
47L6 Nassau
33G2 Nasser, Lake *resr*
11I8 Nässjö
35C6 Nata
53K5 Natal
47I5 Natchez
47I5 Natchitoches
49D4 National City
32D3 Natitingou
53I6 Natividade
31F5 Natori
34D4 Natron, Lake *salt l.*
27J6 Natuna Besar *i.*
40D6 Naturaliste, Cape
40C5 Naturaliste Channel
11M8 Naujoji Akmenė
23J8 Naurskaya
39G2 Nauru
11N10 Navahrudak
17F4 Navan
11P9 Navapolatsk
19F2 Navarra *reg.*
22I5 Navashino
51I5 Navassa Island *terr.*
23G5 Navlya
21M2 Năvodari
26F2 Navoi
46F6 Navojoa
46F7 Navolato
26F4 Nawabshah
26D3 Naxçıvan
21K6 Naxos *i.*
30F3 Nayoro
55D1 Nazaré
33G1 Nazareth
55A2 Nazário
52D6 Nazca
21M6 Nazilli
23J8 Nazran'
34D3 Nazrēt
26E4 Nazwá
35B4 N'dalatando
34C3 Ndélé
33E3 Ndjamena
35C5 Ndola
17F3 Neagh, Lough *l.*
21J5 Nea Liosia
21J6 Neapoli
15D7 Neath
34D3 Nebbi
26E3 Nebitdag
22G4 Nebolchi
46G3 Nebraska *state*
47H3 Nebraska City
54E5 Necochea
19F6 Nédroma
23K5 Neftegorsk
30F1 Neftegorsk
24G4 Neftekamsk
23J7 Neftekumsk
24I3 Nefteyugansk
35B4 Negage
34D3 Negēlē
21J4 Negotino
52G4 Negro *r.*
55A4 Negro *r.*
29E7 Negros *i.*
30B2 Nehe
27J4 Neijiang
30A2 Nei Mongol Zizhiqu *aut. reg.*
52C3 Neiva
34D3 Nek'emtē
22I4 Nekrasovskoye
22G4 Nelidovo
27G5 Nellore
14E5 Nelson
43D5 Nelson
44G5 Nelson
45I4 Nelson *r.*
37J3 Nelspruit
32C3 Néma
11M9 Neman
18F2 Nemours
30G4 Nemuro
30G4 Nemuro-kaikyō *sea chan.*
23F6 Nemyriv
17D5 Nenagh
30B2 Nenjiang
47I4 Neosho
27H4 Nepal
42F1 Nerang
25M4 Nerchinsk
22I4 Nerekhta
55A2 Nerópolis
25N4 Neryungri
16E3 Ness, Loch *l.*
21K4 Nestos *r.*
12J4 Netherlands
51K6 Netherlands Antilles *terr.*
13N4 Neubrandenburg
18H3 Neuchâtel
18H3 Neuchâtel, Lac de *l.*
15I8 Neufchâtel-Hardelot
13L3 Neumünster
13K6 Neunkirchen
13P7 Neunkirchen
54C5 Neuquén
13N4 Neuruppin
13P7 Neusiedler See *l.*
13N4 Neustrelitz
13K5 Neuwied
47I4 Nevada
46D4 Nevada *state*
19E5 Nevada, Sierra *mts*
46C3 Nevada, Sierra *mts*
22F4 Nevel'
30F3 Nevel'sk
30B1 Never
18F3 Nevers
20H3 Nevesinje
23I7 Nevinnomyssk
35D5 Newala
47J4 New Albany
53G2 New Amsterdam
48D2 Newark
48D3 Newark
15G5 Newark-on-Trent
48F2 New Bedford
47L4 New Bern
47K5 Newberry
47I5 New Boston
46H6 New Braunfels
48E2 New Britain
38E2 New Britain *i.*
48D2 New Brunswick
45L5 New Brunswick *prov.*
48D2 Newburgh
15F7 Newbury
48F1 Newburyport
39G4 New Caledonia *terr.*
17G3 Newcastle
37I4 Newcastle
42E4 Newcastle
48A2 New Castle
15E5 Newcastle-under-Lyme
14F4 Newcastle upon Tyne
17C5 Newcastle West
48E2 New City
16E5 New Cumnock
27G4 New Delhi
42E3 New England Range *mts*
15E7 Newent
48B1 Newfane
45M5 Newfoundland *i.*
45M4 Newfoundland and Labrador *prov.*
38E2 New Guinea *i.*
33G3 New Halfa
48F1 New Hampshire *state*
48E2 New Haven
47I5 New Iberia
38F2 New Ireland *i.*
48D3 New Jersey *state*
48B2 New Kensington
45K5 New Liskeard
48E2 New London
40D4 Newman
15H6 Newmarket
48A3 New Martinsville
46F5 New Mexico *state*
47I6 New Orleans
48A2 New Philadelphia
43E4 New Plymouth
15D7 Newport
15E6 Newport
15F8 Newport
46C3 Newport
47I4 Newport
48F2 Newport
49D4 Newport Beach
48C4 Newport News
15G6 Newport Pagnell
15B8 Newquay
47I5 New Roads
48E2 New Rochelle
17F5 New Ross
17F3 Newry
25P2 New Siberia Islands
42C4 New South Wales *state*
48B2 New Stanton
47H4 Newton
47I3 Newton
48D2 Newton
48F1 Newton
15D8 Newton Abbot
16E6 Newton Stewart
15D6 Newtown
46G2 New Town
17G3 Newtownabbey
17G3 Newtownards
17F4 Newtown-mountkennedy
47I3 New Ulm
48E2 New York
48D1 New York *state*
43D5 New Zealand
22I4 Neya
26E4 Neyrīz
26E3 Neyshābūr
32E4 Ngaoundal
33E4 Ngaoundéré
32E3 Nguigmi
32E3 Nguru
37J5 Ngwelezana
29C6 Nha Trang
41I7 Nhill
37J4 Nhlangano
32C3 Niafounké
48B1 Niagara Falls
48B1 Niagara Falls
32D3 Niamey
30A3 Nianzishan
29B7 Nias *i.*
51G6 Nicaragua
51G6 Nicaragua, Lake
20G5 Nicastro
18H5 Nice
49A1 Nice
27I6 Nicobar Islands
33G1 Nicosia
11L9 Nida
13R4 Nidzica
13L4 Nienburg (Weser)
53G2 Nieuw Nickerie
26C3 Niğde
32D3 Niger
32D4 Niger *r.*
32D4 Nigeria
31E5 Niigata
31D6 Niihama
31D6 Niimi
31E5 Niitsu
13J5 Nijmegen
10Q2 Nikel'
23J5 Nikolayevka
23J6 Nikolayevsk
30F1 Nikolayevsk-na-Amure
22J4 Nikol'sk
23G7 Nikopol'
20H3 Nikšić
33G1 Nile *r.*
48A2 Niles
18G5 Nîmes
30C3 Ning'an
28E5 Ningbo
31F4 Ninohe
32C3 Niono
32C3 Nioro
18D3 Niort
45J5 Nipigon, Lake
45K5 Nipissing, Lake
55A1 Niquelândia
27G5 Nirmal
21I3 Niš
20F6 Niscemi
55C3 Niterói
13Q6 Nitra
39J3 Niue *terr.*
10N5 Nivala
27G5 Nizamabad
22K5 Nizhnekamsk
25K4 Nizhneudinsk
24I3 Nizhnevartovsk
25O2 Nizhneyansk
23I5 Nizhniy Lomov
22I4 Nizhniy Novgorod
22L3 Nizhnyaya Omra
24J3 Nizhnyaya Tunguska *r.*
23F6 Nizhyn
35D4 Njombe
10J5 Njurundabommen
32E4 Nkambe
32C4 Nkawkaw
35D5 Nkhata Bay
35D5 Nkhotakota
32D4 Nkongsamba
31C6 Nobeoka
30F4 Noboribetsu
46E5 Nogales
46E5 Nogales
31C6 Nōgata
18E2 Nogent-le-Rotrou
22H5 Noginsk
30F2 Nogliki
34B3 Nola
22K4 Nolinsk
44B3 Nome
30B3 Nong'an
45K5 Noranda
11I6 Norberg
13K4 Norden
13M4 Norderstedt
13M5 Nordhausen
47H3 Norfolk
48C4 Norfolk
39G4 Norfolk Island *terr.*
24J3 Noril'sk
47H4 Norman
53G3 Normandia
18D2 Normandy *reg.*
41I3 Normanton
10L5 Norra Kvarken *strait*
48D2 Norristown
11J7 Norrköping
11K7 Norrtälje
53G6 Nortelândia
14F4 Northallerton
15G6 Northampton
48E1 Northampton
47O4 North Atlantic Ocean
45K5 North Bay
48A2 North Canton
10N1 North Cape
43D2 North Cape
47L4 North Carolina *state*
47K2 North Channel *lake channel*
17G2 North Channel
46G2 North Dakota *state*
15G7 North Downs *hills*
36D5 Northern Cape *prov.*
17F3 Northern Ireland *prov.*
29G6 Northern Mariana Islands *terr.*
40G3 Northern Territory *admin. div.*
13L3 North Frisian Islands
48E2 North Haven
43D4 North Island
48A2 North Kingsville
31B5 North Korea
49E2 North Las Vegas
46G3 North Platte
46G3 North Platte *r.*
16G1 North Ronaldsay Firth *sea chan.*
44H4 North Saskatchewan *r.*
12H2 North Sea
14F3 North Shields
43E4 North Taranaki Bight *b.*
48B1 North Tonawanda
14E4 North Tyne *r.*
16B3 North Uist *i.*
36G4 North West *prov.*
44H3 Northwest Territories *admin. div.*
14E5 Northwich
14G4 North York Moors
44B3 Norton Sound *sea chan.*
47K3 Norwalk
48E2 Norwalk
10E6 Norway
10E3 Norwegian Sea
15I6 Norwich
48D1 Norwich
48E2 Norwich
31F4 Noshiro
35C6 Nosop *watercourse*
36D2 Nossob *watercourse*
11F7 Notodden
45L5 Notre Dame, Monts *mts*
45M5 Notre Dame Bay
15F6 Nottingham
32B2 Nouâdhibou
32B3 Nouakchott
39G4 Nouméa
32C3 Nouna
39G4 Nouvelle Calédonie *i.*
55C3 Nova Friburgo
55C3 Nova Iguaçu
21O1 Nova Kakhovka
55C2 Nova Lima
23F7 Nova Odesa
53J5 Nova Pilão Arcado
55B2 Nova Ponte
20C2 Novara
45L5 Nova Scotia *prov.*
53J5 Nova Sento Sé
49A1 Novato
55A4 Nova Trento
55C2 Nova Venécia
53H6 Nova Xavantino
25P2 Novaya Sibir', Ostrov *i.*
24G2 Novaya Zemlya *is*
21L3 Nova Zagora
19F4 Novelda
13Q7 Nové Zámky
23G6 Novhorod-Sivers'kyy
20C2 Novi Ligure
21I3 Novi Pazar
21L3 Novi Pazar
21H2 Novi Sad
23I6 Novoanninskiy
52F5 Novo Aripuanã
23H7 Novoazovs'k
22J4 Novocheboksarsk
23I7 Novocherkassk
55C2 Novo Cruzeiro
22I2 Novodvinsk
55A5 Novo Hamburgo
23E6 Novohrad-Volyns'kyy
23I6 Novokhopersk
30C2 Novokiyevskiy Uval
23I7 Novokubansk
23K5 Novokuybyshevsk
24J4 Novokuznetsk
20F2 Novo Mesto
23G6 Novomoskovs'k
23H5 Novomoskovsk
23I6 Novonikolayevskiy
23I7 Novopokrovskaya
23H6 Novopskov
23H7 Novorossiysk
22F4 Novorzhev
23H7 Novoshakhtinsk
24J4 Novosibirsk
22F4 Novosokol'niki
23J5 Novospasskoye
23G7 Novotroyits'ke
23F6 Novoukrayinka
23K6 Novouzensk
23E6 Novovolyns'k
23H6 Novovoronezh
23F5 Novozybkov
13P6 Nový Jičín
23H6 Novyy Oskol
24I3 Novyy Urengoy
22L5 Novyy Zay
42E5 Nowra
13R6 Nowy Sącz
13R6 Nowy Targ
24I3 Noyabr'sk
35D5 Nsanje
32D4 Nsukka
34D4 Ntungamo
33G3 Nuba Mountains
33G2 Nubian Desert
51H4 Nueva Gerona
54B5 Nueva Imperial
52C3 Nueva Loja
46G6 Nueva Rosita
50G6 Nueva San Salvador
51I4 Nuevitas
46F5 Nuevo Casas Grandes
46H6 Nuevo Laredo
39I4 Nuku'alofa
26E2 Nukus
40F6 Nullarbor Plain
34B3 Numan
31E6 Numazu
42B6 Numurkah
45J2 Nunavut *admin. div.*
15F6 Nuneaton
44B4 Nunivak Island
19C3 Nuñomoral
20C4 Nuoro
34E1 Nuqrah
13M6 Nuremberg
23K5 Nurlat
10P5 Nurmes
10M5 Nurmo
45M3 Nuuk
36E7 Nuweveldberge *mts*
24H3 Nyagan'
33F3 Nyala
35D5 Nyamtumbo
22I3 Nyandoma
35D4 Nyasa, Lake
11O10 Nyasvizh
11G9 Nyborg
11I8 Nybro
34D4 Nyeri
23D7 Nyíregyháza
11G9 Nykøbing
11G9 Nykøbing Sjælland
11J7 Nyköping
11J7 Nynäshamn
42C3 Nyngan
18H3 Nyon
13P5 Nysa
35C4 Nyunzu
25M3 Nyurba
35D4 Nzega
32C4 Nzérékoré

O

46□ Oahu *i.*
42E1 Oakey
15G6 Oakham
49A2 Oakland
46C3 Oakridge
48B1 Oakville
43C7 Oamaru
50E5 Oaxaca
24H3 Ob' *r.*
31D6 Obama
16D4 Oban
42D4 Oberon
13N6 Oberpfälzer Wald *mts*
53G4 Óbidos
30F4 Obihiro
23J7 Obil'noye
30C2 Obluch'ye
23H5 Obninsk
34C3 Obo
34E2 Obock
23H6 Oboyan'
21I2 Obrenovac
24I3 Obskaya Guba *sea chan.*
32C4 Obuasi
22K3 Ob''yachevo
47K6 Ocala
19E4 Ocaña
52D2 Ocaña
52C3 Occidental, Cordillera *mts*
52D7 Occidental, Cordillera *mts*
48D3 Ocean City
49D4 Oceanside
21N1 Ochakiv
23I8 Och'amch'ire
16F4 Ochil Hills
15H9 Octeville-sur-Mer
10□1 Ódáðahraun *lava field*
31F4 Ōdate
31E6 Odawara
11E6 Odda
21L5 Ödemiș
11G9 Odense
13O3 Oderbucht *b.*
21N1 Odesa
46G5 Odessa
32C4 Odienné
22H5 Odintsovo
13Q6 Odra *r.*
53J5 Oeiras
23I8 Of
32D4 Offa
13L5 Offenbach am Main
13K6 Offenburg
31E5 Oga
31E6 Ōgaki
46G3 Ogallala
32D4 Ogbomosho
46E3 Ogden
11N8 Ogre
48A3 Ohio *r.*
48A2 Ohio *state*
21I4 Ohrid
21I4 Ohrid, Lake
48B2 Oil City
31C6 Ōita
46G6 Ojinaga
31E5 Ojiya
54C3 Ojos del Salado, Nevado *mt.*
23I4 Oka *r.*
35C5 Okavango Delta *swamp*
31E5 Okaya
31D6 Okayama
31E6 Okazaki
47K6 Okeechobee, Lake
15C8 Okehampton
30F1 Okha
25P4 Okhotsk
30G3 Okhotsk, Sea of
23G6 Okhtyrka
31B8 Okinawa-shotō *is*
46H4 Oklahoma *state*
47H4 Oklahoma City
47H4 Okmulgee
22G5 Okovskiy Les *for.*
22I3 Oktyabr'skiy
23I7 Oktyabr'skiy
24G4 Oktyabr'skiy
25Q4 Oktyabr'skiy
25K2 Oktyabr'skoy Revolyutsii, Ostrov *i.*
22G4 Okulovka
32D4 Okuta
11J8 Öland *i.*
54D5 Olavarría
13P5 Oława
20C4 Olbia
13L4 Oldenburg
14E5 Oldham
17D6 Old Head of Kinsale
48B1 Olean
13S3 Olecko
25N3 Olekminsk
23G6 Oleksandriya
10R2 Olenegorsk
22G4 Olenino
23E6 Olevs'k
19C5 Olhão
36D6 Olifants *r.*
36E7 Olifants *r.*
37J3 Olifants *r.*
53L5 Olinda
19F4 Oliva
54C3 Oliva, Cordillera de *mts*
55C1 Oliveira dos Brejinhos
52C5 Olmos
15G6 Olney
48C3 Olney
11I8 Olofström
13P6 Olomouc
22G3 Olonets
18D5 Oloron-Ste-Marie
19H2 Olot
25M4 Olovyannaya
13R4 Olsztyn
18H3 Olten
21L2 Oltenița
46C2 Olympia
21J4 Olympus, Mount
17E3 Omagh
47H3 Omaha
36D2 Omaheke *admin. reg.*
26E5 Oman
26E4 Oman, Gulf of
33G3 Omdurman
33G3 Om Hajēr
31E6 Ōmiya
24I4 Omsk
25Q3 Omsukchan
31C6 Ōmura
22L4 Omutninsk
54D4 Oncativo
35B5 Ondjiva
32D4 Ondo
27K2 Öndörhaan
22H3 Onega
22H3 Onega *r.*
22G3 Onega, Lake
24E3 Onega, Lake
48D1 Oneida
48D1 Oneonta
21L1 Onești
22G2 Onezhskaya Guba *g.*
31B5 Ongjin
27H5 Ongole
32D4 Onitsha
31D6 Onomichi
49D3 Ontario
48A1 Ontario *prov.*
48C1 Ontario, Lake
53G2 Onverwacht
22K4 Oparino
13P6 Opava
47J5 Opelika
47I5 Opelousas
11P8 Opochka
13P5 Opole
19B3 Oporto
35B5 Opuwo
21I1 Oradea
19F6 Oran
54D2 Orán
30C4 Ŏrang
18G4 Orange
42D4 Orange
47I5 Orange
49D4 Orange
36C5 Orange *r.*
47K5 Orangeburg
50G5 Orange Walk
36C5 Oranjemund
51J6 Oranjestad
21J2 Orăștie
42D6 Orbost
23H8 Ordu
32D4 Ore
11I7 Örebro
46C3 Oregon *state*
46C2 Oregon City
22H5 Orekhovo-Zuyevo
23H5 Orel
24G4 Orenburg
11H9 Öresund *strait*
15I6 Orford Ness *hd*
21M5 Orhaneli
21M4 Orhangazi
22K4 Orichi
52D2 Oriental, Cordillera *mts*
52E6 Oriental, Cordillera *mts*
19F4 Orihuela
23G7 Orikhiv
11N6 Orimattila
52F2 Orinoco *r.*
20C5 Oristano
11N6 Orivesi
53G4 Oriximiná
50E5 Orizaba
55A2 Orizona
37H4 Orkney
16F1 Orkney *is*
55B3 Orlândia
47K6 Orlando
55A5 Orleaes
18E3 Orléans
22K4 Orlov
23I7 Orlovskiy
14E5 Ormskirk
10K5 Örnsköldsvik
32C3 Orodara
29E7 Oroquieta
21I1 Orosháza
46C4 Oroville
30A2 Orqohan
23F5 Orsha
22J4 Orshanka
24G4 Orsk
10E5 Ørsta
18D5 Orthez
20F3 Ortona
52E7 Oruro
20E3 Orvieto
31D6 Ōsaka
11H8 Osby
27G2 Osh
35B5 Oshakati
45K5 Oshawa
47J3 Oshkosh
32D4 Oshogbo
20H2 Osijek
20E3 Osimo
37J4 Osizweni
11J8 Oskarshamn
11G7 Oslo
11G7 Oslofjorden *sea chan.*
23G8 Osmancık
21M4 Osmaneli
13L4 Osnabrück
19D2 Osorno
54B6 Osorno
46D2 Osoyoos
11D6 Osøyri
13J5 Oss
48E2 Ossining
22G4 Ostashkov
12I5 Ostend
10I5 Östersund
13Q6 Ostrava
13Q4 Ostróda
23H6 Ostrogozhsk
11P8 Ostrov
22I4 Ostrovskoye
23D6 Ostrowiec Świętokrzyski
13R4 Ostrów Mazowiecka
13P5 Ostrów Wielkopolski
48C1 Oswego
15D6 Oswestry
43C7 Otago Peninsula
43E5 Otaki
30F4 Otaru
31F5 Ōtawara
11O7 Otepää
35B6 Otjiwarongo
36C1 Otjozondjupa *admin. reg.*
14F5 Otley
23K5 Otradnyy
20H4 Otranto, Strait of
31D6 Ōtsu
45K5 Ottawa
47H4 Ottawa
47J3 Ottawa
47I3 Ottumwa
42A7 Otway, Cape
47I5 Ouachita Mountains
33F3 Ouaddaï *reg.*
32C3 Ouagadougou
32C3 Ouahigouya
32D3 Ouargaye
32D1 Ouargla
32C1 Ouarzazate
36F7 Oudtshoorn
32C1 Oued Zem
20B6 Oued Zénati
34B3 Ouesso
19D6 Ouezzane
19F6 Oujda
10N4 Oulainen
19I6 Ouled Djellal
19G5 Ouled Farès
10N4 Oulu
10O4 Oulujärvi *l.*
10N4 Oulunsalo
20B7 Oum el Bouaghi
15G6 Oundle
19C2 Ourense
53J5 Ouricurí
55A3 Ourinhos
55C3 Ouro Preto
14G5 Ouse *r.*
15H8 Ouse *r.*
16B3 Outer Hebrides *is*
49C4 Outer Santa Barbara Channel
46F1 Outlook
10P5 Outokumpu
41I7 Ouyen
54B4 Ovalle
19B3 Ovar
19D2 Oviedo
23F6 Ovruch
34B4 Owando
31E6 Owase
47I3 Owatonna
48C1 Owego
47J4 Owensboro
49D2 Owens Lake
45J5 Owen Sound
38E2 Owen Stanley Range *mts*
32D4 Owerri
32D4 Owo
10□1 Öxarfjörður *b.*
11J7 Oxelösund
15F7 Oxford
47J5 Oxford
49C3 Oxnard
31E5 Oyama
34B3 Oyem
32D4 Oyo
18G3 Oyonnax
47J5 Ozark
47I4 Ozark Plateau
47I4 Ozarks, Lake of the
25Q4 Ozernovskiy
11M9 Ozersk
30F3 Ozerskiy
23H5 Ozery
23K6 Ozinki

P

45N3 Paamiut
36D7 Paarl
13Q5 Pabianice
27H4 Pabna
52C5 Pacasmayo
20F6 Pachino
50E4 Pachuca
49B2 Pacific Grove
29C8 Padang
22G3 Padany
13L5 Paderborn
15C8 Padstow
20D2 Padua
47J4 Paducah
20F2 Pag
20F2 Pag *i.*
29E7 Pagadian
11N7 Paide
15D8 Paignton
11N6 Päijänne *l.*
11M6 Paimio
48A2 Painesville
16E5 Paisley
52B5 Paita
52F3 Pakaraima Mountains
52G3 Pakaraima Mountains
25R3 Pakhachi
26F3 Pakistan
11M9 Pakruojis
20H1 Paks
29C6 Pakxé
33E4 Pala
18F2 Palaiseau
25Q4 Palana
27G4 Palanpur
37H2 Palapye
25Q3 Palatka
29F7 Palau
29D7 Palawan *i.*
22I4 Palekh
29C8 Palembang
54B6 Palena
19D2 Palencia
20E5 Palermo
47H5 Palestine
27G5 Palghat
55A4 Palhoca
27G4 Pali
7 Palikir
27G6 Palk Strait
23J6 Pallasovka
43E5 Palliser, Cape
19H4 Palma de Mallorca
53K5 Palmares
55A5 Palmares do Sul
55A4 Palmas
32C4 Palmas, Cape
49C3 Palmdale
55A4 Palmeira
54F3 Palmeira das Missões
53K5 Palmeira dos Índios
53J5 Palmeirais
39J3 Palmerston *atoll*
43E5 Palmerston North
20F5 Palmi
52C3 Palmira
49D4 Palm Springs
49A2 Palo Alto
29E8 Palopo
29D8 Palu
18E5 Pamiers
27G3 Pamir *mts*
47L4 Pamlico Sound *sea chan.*
54D5 Pampas *reg.*
19F2 Pamplona
52D2 Pamplona
21N4 Pamukova
21K3 Panagyurishte
27G5 Panaji
51H7 Panama
51I7 Panama, Gulf of
51I7 Panama Canal
47J5 Panama City
51I7 Panama City
29E6 Panay *i.*
21I2 Pančevo
11N9 Panevėžys
29D8 Pangkalanbuun
29C8 Pangkalpinang
45L3 Pangnirtung
10Q5 Pankakoski
55A3 Panorama
30B4 Panshi
50E4 Pánuco
27J4 Panzhihua
34B3 Paoua
20G1 Pápa
43E3 Papakura
50E4 Papantla
16□ Papa Stour *i.*
13K4 Papenburg
33G1 Paphos
38E2 Papua, Gulf of
41J1 Papua New Guinea
15C8 Par
55B2 Pará *r.*
53I4 Pará, Rio do *r.*
40D4 Paraburdoo
55B2 Paracatu
29D6 Paracel Islands
21I3 Paraćin
53K4 Paracuru
55B2 Pará de Minas
46C4 Paradise
53I4 Paragominas
47I4 Paragould
55A3 Paraguaçu Paulista
54E2 Paraguay
54E3 Paraguay *r.*
53I6 Paraíso do Norte
55B3 Paraisópolis
32D4 Parakou
53G2 Paramaribo
55C1 Paramirim
48D2 Paramus
54D4 Paraná
55B1 Paranã
53H8 Paraná *r.*
55A1 Paraná *r.*
55A4 Paraná *state*
55A4 Paranaguá
55A2 Paranaíba
55A4 Paranapiacaba, Serra *mts*
54F2 Paranavaí
55B2 Paraopeba
55C1 Paratinga
55A2 Paraúna
27G5 Parbhani
13M4 Parchim
13O5 Pardubice
52F6 Parecis, Serra dos *hills*
29D8 Parepare
11M6 Pargas
51L6 Paria, Gulf of
53G4 Parintins
18F2 Paris
47H5 Paris
11M5 Parkano
48A3 Parkersburg
42D4 Parkes
20D2 Parma
48A2 Parma
53J4 Parnaíba
11N7 Pärnu
42A3 Paroo *watercourse*
21K6 Paros
21K6 Paros *i.*
54B5 Parral
42E4 Parramatta
46G6 Parras
45G2 Parry Channel
45G2 Parry Islands
47H4 Parsons
18D3 Parthenay
30D4 Partizansk
49C3 Pasadena
47J5 Pascagoula
21L1 Pașcani
23H7 Pashkovskiy
54E4 Paso de los Toros
49B3 Paso Robles
48D2 Passaic
55B3 Passa Tempo
13N6 Passau
54F3 Passo Fundo
55B3 Passos
11O9 Pastavy
52C3 Pasto
53J5 Pastos Bons
11N8 Pasvalys
54B8 Patagonia *reg.*
48D2 Paterson
27H4 Patna
54F3 Pato Branco
53K5 Patos
54F4 Patos, Lagoa dos *l.*
55B2 Patos de Minas
21I5 Patras
55B2 Patrocínio
48B2 Patton
53K5 Patu
18D5 Pau
52E5 Pauini
53K5 Paulo Afonso
55C2 Pavão
20C2 Pavia
21K3 Pavlikeni
27G1 Pavlodar
23G6 Pavlohrad
23J5 Pavlovka
22I5 Pavlovo
23I6 Pavlovsk
23H7 Pavlovskaya
48F2 Pawtucket
29C8 Payakumbuh
46D3 Payette
54E4 Paysandú
23I8 Pazar
21K3 Pazardzhik
20E2 Pazin
48F1 Peabody
44G4 Peace *r.*
46H6 Pearsall
45I2 Peary Channel
21I3 Peć
55C2 Peçanha
10Q2 Pechenga
22M2 Pechora
22L1 Pechora *r.*
22L1 Pechorskaya Guba *b.*
11O8 Pechory
46G5 Pecos
46G6 Pecos *r.*
20H1 Pécs
51J5 Pedernales
55C1 Pedra Azul
55B3 Pedregulho
53J4 Pedreiras
54E2 Pedro Juan Caballero
16F5 Peebles
48E2 Peekskill
43D6 Pegasus Bay
27I5 Pegu
54D5 Pehuajó
11O7 Peipus, Lake
53I6 Peixe
53H6 Peixoto de Azevedo
32D3 Pekinga
21J6 Peloponnese *admin. reg.*
54F4 Pelotas
35E5 Pemba
15C7 Pembroke
45K5 Pembroke
55A3 Penápolis
15D7 Penarth
54A7 Penas, Golfo de *g.*
46D2 Pendleton
55A4 Penha
19B4 Peniche
16F5 Penicuik
29C7 Peninsular Malaysia
48B2 Penn Hills
18H4 Pennine, Alpi *mts*
14E4 Pennines *hills*
48D2 Pennsburg
48D3 Pennsville
48B2 Pennsylvania *state*
48C1 Penn Yan
51H7 Penonomé
14E4 Penrith
42E4 Penrith
47J5 Pensacola
44G5 Penticton
16F2 Pentland Firth *sea chan.*
16F5 Pentland Hills
23J5 Penza
15B8 Penzance
47J3 Peoria
55B2 Perdizes
52C3 Pereira
55A3 Pereira Barreto
23E6 Peremyshlyany
22H4 Pereslavl'-Zalesskiy
30D3 Pereyaslavka
23F6 Pereyaslav-Khmel'nyts'kyy
54D4 Pergamino
54C2 Perico
18E4 Périgueux
24G4 Perm'
21J3 Pernik
18F5 Perpignan
15B8 Perranporth
49D4 Perris
47K5 Perry
46G4 Perryton
47J4 Perryville
16F4 Perth
40D6 Perth
48D2 Perth Amboy
52D6 Peru
20E3 Perugia
23F6 Pervomays'k
23I5 Pervomaysk
23I5 Pervomayskiy
23H6 Pervomays'kyy
20E3 Pesaro
20F3 Pescara
23I7 Peschanokopskoye
27G3 Peshawar
21I4 Peshkopi
21K3 Peshtera
20F1 Pesnica
18D4 Pessac
22G4 Pestovo
23K5 Pestravka
49A1 Petaluma
50D5 Petatlán
15G6 Peterborough
41H6 Peterborough
45K5 Peterborough
48F1 Peterborough
16H3 Peterhead
14F4 Peterlee
48C4 Petersburg
15G7 Petersfield
44C3 Petersville
50G4 Peto
47K2 Petoskey
21J4 Petrich
53J5 Petrolina
55A2 Petrolina de Goiás
27F1 Petropavlovsk
25Q4 Petropavlovsk-Kamchatskiy
55C3 Petrópolis
21J2 Petroșani
23J5 Petrovsk
25L4 Petrovsk-Zabaykal'skiy
22G3 Petrozavodsk
24H4 Petukhovo
22H5 Petushki
25S3 Pevek
13P6 Pezinok
13L6 Pforzheim
37H5 Phahameng
37J2 Phalaborwa
29B7 Phangnga
29C6 Phan Rang
29C6 Phan Thiêt
29C7 Phatthalung
47J5 Phenix City
29B6 Phet Buri
48D3 Philadelphia
29E6 Philippines
29E6 Philippine Sea
37H4 Phiritona
29C6 Phitsanulok
29C6 Phnom Penh
46E5 Phoenix
39I2 Phoenix Islands
28C5 Phôngsali
29C6 Phrae
29B7 Phuket
20C2 Piacenza
21L1 Piatra Neamț
15J9 Picardie *admin. reg.*
18E2 Picardy *reg.*
15F9 Picauville
47J5 Picayune
54D2 Pichanal
54B4 Pichilemu
14G4 Pickering
53J5 Picos
54C7 Pico Truncado
42E5 Picton
55B3 Piedade

46G6 Piedras Negras
10O5 Pieksämäki
10P5 Pielinen *l.*
46G3 Pierre
37J5 Pietermaritzburg
37I2 Pietersburg
37J3 Pigg's Peak
10P6 Pihlajavesi *l.*
22G4 Pikalevo
47K4 Pikeville
13P4 Piła
54E3 Pilar
54E4 Pilar
22J5 Pil'na
52F6 Pimenta Bueno
54E5 Pinamar
51H4 Pinar del Río
21L4 Pinarhisar
52C4 Piñas
13R5 Pińczów
55C1 Pindaí
55B3 Pindamonhangaba
21I5 Pindus Mountains
47I5 Pine Bluff
22I2 Pinega
20B2 Pinerolo
37J5 Pinetown
27K3 Pingdingshan
27J4 Pingxiang
27K4 Pingxiang
55B3 Pinhal
53I4 Pinheiro
40D6 Pinjarra
11O10 Pinsk
13R5 Pionki
13O5 Piotrków Trybunalski
55A2 Piracanjuba
55B3 Piracicaba
55B3 Piraçununga
53J4 Piracuruca
21J6 Piraeus
55A4 Piraí do Sul
55A3 Piraju
55A3 Pirajuí
53H7 Piranhas
53K5 Piranhas *r.*
55B2 Pirapora
55A1 Pirenópolis
55A2 Pires do Rio
53J4 Piripiri
20D3 Pisa
52C6 Pisco
13O6 Písek
54C3 Pissis, Cerro
50G4 Pisté
20D3 Pistoia
32B3 Pita
55A4 Pitanga
55B2 Pitangui
6 Pitcairn Islands *terr.*
10L4 Piteå
23J6 Piterka
21K2 Pitești
22F3 Pitkyaranta
16F4 Pitlochry
48B2 Pittsburgh
48E1 Pittsfield
42E1 Pittsworth
55B3 Piumhí
52B5 Piura
20F2 Pivka
49C3 Pixley
49B1 Placerville
52E6 Plácido de Castro
48F2 Plainfield
46G5 Plainview
55B1 Planaltina
55A3 Planura
47I5 Plaquemine
19C3 Plasencia
52D2 Plato
46H3 Platte *r.*
47M3 Plattsburgh
13N5 Plauen
23H5 Plavsk
52B4 Playas
48D3 Pleasantville
43F3 Plenty, Bay of *g.*
22I3 Plesetsk
21K3 Pleven
21H3 Pljevlja
13O4 Płock
21L2 Ploiești
21K3 Plovdiv
11L9 Plungė
15C8 Plymouth
47J3 Plymouth
48F2 Plymouth
51L5 Plymouth
15D6 Plynlimon *hill*
13N6 Plzeň
32C3 Pô
20E2 Po *r.*
46E3 Pocatello
23E6 Pochayiv
23G5 Pochep
23J5 Pochinki
23G5 Pochinok
55C1 Poções
53G7 Poconé
55B3 Poços de Caldas
23H6 Podgorenskiy
21H3 Podgorica
24J4 Podgornoye
23H5 Podol'sk
22G3 Podporozh'ye
36D5 Pofadder
23G5 Pogar
20D3 Poggibonsi
21I4 Pogradec
31C5 P'ohang
51L5 Pointe-à-Pitre
35B4 Pointe-Noire
48D2 Point Pleasant
18E3 Poitiers
27G4 Pokaran
30C4 Pokhara
25N3 Pokrovsk
23H7 Pokrovskoye
19D2 Pola de Siero
13O4 Poland
11P9 Polatsk
27F3 Pol-e Khomrī
11L9 Polessk
13O4 Police
23F6 Polis'ke
13P5 Polkowice
23H7 Polohy
23E6 Polonne
23G6 Poltava
11O7 Põlva
10R2 Polyarnyy
25S3 Polyarnyy
10R3 Polyarnyye Zori
21J4 Polygyros
53K5 Pombal
20E4 Pomezia
49D3 Pomona
21L3 Pomorie
13O3 Pomorska, Zatoka *b.*
20F4 Pompei
55A3 Pompéia
22J4 Ponazyrevo
47H4 Ponca City
51K5 Ponce
27G5 Pondicherry
19C2 Ponferrada
55A4 Ponta Grossa
55A3 Pontal
55A2 Pontalina
54E2 Ponta Porã
14F5 Pontefract
55C3 Ponte Nova
53G7 Pontes-e-Lacerda
19B2 Pontevedra
47J3 Pontiac
47K3 Pontiac
29C8 Pontianak
18F2 Pontoise
15D7 Pontypool
15D7 Pontypridd
15F8 Poole
52E7 Poopó, Lago de *l.*
52C3 Popayán
47I4 Poplar Bluff
50E5 Popocatépetl, Volcán *vol.*
35B4 Popokabaka
21L3 Popovo
13R6 Poprad
48C4 Poquoson
55A1 Porangatu
27F4 Porbandar
20E2 Poreč
55A3 Porecatu
23J5 Poretskoye
11L6 Pori
43E5 Porirua
11P8 Porkhov
52F1 Porlamar
21J6 Poros
22G3 Porosozero
10N1 Porsangen *sea chan.*
11F7 Porsgrunn
17F3 Portadown
17G3 Portaferry
47J3 Portage
48B2 Portage
45I5 Portage la Prairie
46C2 Port Alberni
19C4 Portalegre
46G5 Portales
46C2 Port Angeles
51I5 Port Antonio
17E4 Portarlington
47I6 Port Arthur
41H6 Port Augusta
51J5 Port-au-Prince
27I5 Port Blair
19H2 Portbou
43C7 Port Chalmers
47K6 Port Charlotte
51J5 Port-de-Paix
41J3 Port Douglas
55C1 Porteirinha
53H4 Portel
37G7 Port Elizabeth
49C2 Porterville
34A4 Port-Gentil
16E5 Port Glasgow
32D4 Port Harcourt
15D7 Porthcawl
40D4 Port Hedland
15B8 Porthleven
15C6 Porthmadog
49C3 Port Hueneme
47K3 Port Huron
19B5 Portimão
41I7 Portland
42D4 Portland
46C2 Portland
47M3 Portland
18F5 Port-la-Nouvelle
17E4 Portlaoise
47H6 Port Lavaca
41H6 Port Lincoln
32B4 Port Loko
7 Port Louis
42F3 Port Macquarie
41J1 Port Moresby
36C5 Port Nolloth
55A5 Porto Alegre
35B5 Porto Amboim
55A4 Porto Belo
53H4 Porto de Moz
53G7 Porto Esperidião
53I5 Porto Franco
51L6 Port of Spain
20E2 Portogruaro
20D2 Portomaggiore
53I6 Porto Nacional
32D4 Porto-Novo
32□ Porto Novo
55D2 Porto Seguro
20C4 Porto Torres
55A4 Porto União
18I6 Porto-Vecchio
52F5 Porto Velho
52B4 Portoviejo
42B7 Port Phillip Bay
41H6 Port Pirie
16C3 Portree
17F2 Portrush
33G1 Port Said
37J6 Port Shepstone
15F8 Portsmouth
47K4 Portsmouth
48C4 Portsmouth
48F1 Portsmouth
47J6 Port St Joe
33G3 Port Sudan
15D7 Port Talbot
19C4 Portugal
39G3 Port Vila
54B8 Porvenir
11N6 Porvoo
54E3 Posadas
22H4 Poshekhon'ye
29E8 Poso
36F5 Postmasburg
55C2 Poté
20F4 Potenza
37I3 Potgietersrus
23I8 P'ot'i
55D1 Potiraguá
32E3 Potiskum
48C3 Potomac *r.*
52E7 Potosí
13N4 Potsdam
15G7 Potters Bar
48D2 Pottstown
48C2 Pottsville
48E2 Poughkeepsie
14E5 Poulton-le-Fylde
55B3 Pouso Alegre
29C6 Poŭthĭsăt
13Q6 Považská Bystrica
22G3 Povenets
19B3 Póvoa de Varzim
23I6 Povorino
49D4 Poway
46E4 Powell, Lake *resr*
44F5 Powell River
53H7 Poxoréu
30C2 Poyarkovo
21I2 Požarevac
50E4 Poza Rica
20G2 Požega
21I3 Požega
13P4 Poznań
54E2 Pozo Colorado
20F4 Pozzuoli
13O6 Prachatice
29B6 Prachuap Khiri Khan
55D2 Prado
13O5 Prague
32□ Praia
53H4 Prainha
47I3 Prairie du Chien
55A2 Prata
55A2 Prata *r.*
20D3 Prato
46H4 Pratt
22I4 Prechistoye
11O8 Preiļi
13N4 Prenzlau
13P6 Přerov
46E5 Prescott
21I3 Preševo
54D3 Presidencia Roque Sáenz Peña
53J5 Presidente Dutra
55B2 Presidente Olegário
55A3 Presidente Prudente
55A3 Presidente Venceslau
23D6 Prešov
21I4 Prespa, Lake
47N2 Presque Isle
14E5 Preston
16E5 Prestwick
37I3 Pretoria
21I5 Preveza
44A4 Pribilof Islands
21H3 Priboj
46E4 Price
11L8 Priekule
11N8 Priekuļi
11M9 Prienai
13Q6 Prievidza
20G2 Prijedor
21H3 Prijepolje
21I4 Prilep
30D3 Primorskiy Kray *admin. div.*
23H7 Primorsko-Akhtarsk
44H4 Prince Albert
45K3 Prince Charles Island
45L5 Prince Edward Island *prov.*
44F4 Prince George
45I2 Prince of Wales Island
44E4 Prince Rupert
41I2 Princess Charlotte Bay
46C2 Princeton
48A4 Princeton
48D2 Princeton
44D3 Prince William Sound *b.*
11Q6 Priozersk
23F6 Pripet *r.*
23E6 Pripet Marshes
21I3 Priština
18G4 Privas
20F2 Privlaka
22I4 Privolzhsk
23J6 Privolzhskiy
23K5 Privolzh'ye
23I7 Priyutnoye
21I3 Prizren
53G3 Professor van Blommestein Meer *resr*
30C2 Progress
23J8 Prokhladnyy
24J4 Prokop'yevsk
21I3 Prokuplje
23I7 Proletarsk
55A3 Promissão
53K6 Propriá
21L3 Provadiya
18G5 Provence *reg.*
48F2 Providence
25T3 Provideniya
46E3 Provo
55A4 Prudentópolis
13R4 Pruszków
23F7 Prut *r.*
23G6 Pryluky
23H7 Prymors'k
23D6 Przemyśl
11P8 Pskov
11O7 Pskov, Lake
11P8 Pskovskaya Oblast' *admin. div.*
21I4 Ptolemaïda
20F1 Ptuj
52D5 Pucallpa
22I4 Puchezh
31B5 Puch'ŏn
22H3 Pudozh
14F5 Pudsey
50E5 Puebla
46G4 Pueblo
19D5 Puente-Genil
50E5 Puerto Ángel
51H7 Puerto Armuelles
52E2 Puerto Ayacucho
52□ Puerto Baquerizo Moreno
50G5 Puerto Barrios
52E1 Puerto Cabello
51H6 Puerto Cabezas
52E2 Puerto Carreño
52C4 Puerto Francisco de Orellana
52E3 Puerto Inírida
51H5 Puerto Lempira
51H6 Puerto Limón
19D4 Puertollano
54C6 Puerto Madryn
52E6 Puerto Maldonado
54B6 Puerto Montt
54B8 Puerto Natales
46E5 Puerto Peñasco
51J5 Puerto Plata
29D7 Puerto Princesa
54E3 Puerto Rico
51K5 Puerto Rico *terr.*
54C8 Puerto Santa Cruz
52C6 Puerto Supe
50C4 Puerto Vallarta
23K5 Pugachev
43C7 Pukaki, Lake
31C4 Pukch'ŏng
20E2 Pula
48A4 Pulaski
46D2 Pullman
27G5 Pune
30C4 P'ungsan
52D7 Puno
54D5 Punta Alta
54B8 Punta Arenas
54F5 Punta del Este
50G5 Punta Gorda
51H6 Puntarenas
27H5 Puri
52F4 Purus *r.*
30C4 Puryŏng
31C6 Pusan
23H5 Pushchino
11Q7 Pushkin
11P8 Pushkinskiye Gory
22F4 Pustoshka
28D5 Putian
29C7 Putrajaya
52D4 Putumayo *r.*
15C6 Pwllheli
10Q4 Pyaozerskiy
23I7 Pyatigorsk
23G6 P''yatykhatky
27I5 Pyè
23F5 Pyetrykaw
27I5 Pyinmana
15D7 Pyle
21I6 Pylos
30B4 Pyŏktong
31B5 P'yŏnggang
31B5 P'yŏngsong
31B5 P'yŏngt'aek
31B5 P'yŏngyang
19H2 Pyrenees *mts*
21I6 Pyrgos
23G6 Pyryatyn
13O4 Pyrzyce
11O8 Pytalovo

Q

37I6 Qacha's Nek
27I3 Qaidam Pendi *basin*
45N3 Qaqortoq
34F1 Qatar
33F2 Qattara Depression
23J8 Qax
23J8 Qazax
33H1 Qazvīn
45M3 Qeqertarsuup Tunua *b.*
33H1 Qeydār
30B3 Qian'an
27I3 Qilian Shan *mts*
33G2 Qinā
30B3 Qing'an
28E4 Qingdao
30B3 Qinggang
30B4 Qingyuan
27K3 Qinhuangdao
27J3 Qin Ling *mts*
27J4 Qinzhou
27K5 Qionghai
30A3 Qiqihar
30C3 Qitaihe
26E3 Qom
33H1 Qorveh
29C6 Quang Ngai
15D7 Quantock Hills
44H4 Qu'Appelle *r.*
20C5 Quartu Sant'Elena
42D5 Queanbeyan
45K5 Québec
45K4 Québec *prov.*
44E4 Queen Charlotte Islands
44F4 Queen Charlotte Sound *sea chan.*
45H2 Queen Elizabeth Islands
56C6 Queen Maud Land *reg.*
42B7 Queenscliff
42B1 Queensland *state*
41J8 Queenstown
43B7 Queenstown
35D5 Quelimane
50D4 Querétaro
26F3 Quetta
50F6 Quetzaltenango
29E6 Quezon City
35B5 Quibala
52C2 Quibdó
52D6 Quillabamba
52E7 Quillacollo
54E4 Quilmes
27G6 Quilon
54B4 Quilpué
35B4 Quimbele
18B3 Quimper
18C3 Quimperlé
47I4 Quincy
48F1 Quincy
29C6 Qui Nhơn
19F3 Quinto
42E3 Quirindi
55A2 Quirinópolis
54D3 Quitilipi
52C4 Quito
53K4 Quixadá
53K5 Quixeramobim
27J4 Qujing
41H6 Quorn
27F3 Qŭrghonteppa
28D5 Quzhou

R

10N4 Raahe
16C3 Raasay *i.*
16C3 Raasay, Sound of *sea chan.*
29D8 Raba
32C1 Rabat
38F2 Rabaul
22G2 Rabocheostrovsk
29C7 Rach Gia
13Q5 Racibórz
47J3 Racine
23E7 Rădăuti
47J4 Radcliff
48A4 Radford
21K3 Radnevo
13R5 Radom
21J3 Radomir
13Q5 Radomsko
11N9 Radun'
11M9 Radviliškis
23E6 Radyvyliv
54D4 Rafaela
26E3 Rafsanjān
20F6 Ragusa
29E8 Raha
23F5 Rahachow
27G4 Rahimyar Khan
27G5 Raichur
27H4 Raigarh
46C2 Rainier, Mount *vol.*
27H4 Raipur
11M6 Raisio
27H5 Rajahmundry
27G4 Rajkot
27H4 Rajshahi
23E6 Rakhiv
23G6 Rakitnoye
21K3 Rakovski
11O7 Rakvere
47L4 Raleigh
15C8 Rame Head
21L2 Râmnicu Sărat
21K2 Râmnicu Vâlcea
23H6 Ramon'
49D4 Ramona
37G3 Ramotswa
27G4 Rampur
14C4 Ramsey
48D2 Ramsey
15I7 Ramsgate
11N9 Ramygala
27H4 Ranaghat
54B4 Rancagua
55A3 Rancharia
27H4 Ranchi
17F3 Randalstown
11G8 Randers
10M4 Råneå
27I5 Rangoon
27H4 Rangpur
16E4 Rannoch, L.
29B7 Ranong
29B7 Rantauprapat
20C2 Rapallo
46G3 Rapid City
11N7 Rapla
6 Rarotonga *i.*
34D2 Ras Dejen *mt.*
11M9 Raseiniai
26D3 Rasht
11P9 Rasony
23I5 Rasskazovo
37I4 Ratanda
29B6 Rat Buri
13N4 Rathenow
17F3 Rathfriland
17F2 Rathlin Island
17D5 Rathluirc
27G5 Ratnagiri
23E6 Ratne
46G4 Raton
55C3 Raul Soares
11L6 Rauma
27H4 Raurkela
20E2 Ravenna
48A2 Ravenna
13L7 Ravensburg
27G3 Rawalpindi
13P5 Rawicz
46F3 Rawlins
54C6 Rawson
27H5 Rayagada
30C2 Raychikhinsk
15H7 Rayleigh
42E4 Raymond Terrace
46H6 Raymondville
21L3 Razgrad
21J4 Razlog
15G7 Reading
48D2 Reading
33F2 Rebiana Sand Sea *des.*
40E6 Recherche, Archipelago of the *is*
23F5 Rechytsa
53L5 Recife
37G8 Recife, Cape
13K5 Recklinghausen
54E3 Reconquista
47I5 Red *r.*
48D2 Red Bank
46C3 Red Bluff
14F4 Redcar
41I6 Red Cliffs
44G4 Red Deer
46C3 Redding
15F6 Redditch
53H5 Redenção
49D3 Redlands
47H3 Red Oak
49C4 Redondo Beach
34D1 Red Sea
47I3 Red Wing
49A2 Redwood City
17E4 Ree, Lough *l.*
49C2 Reedley
13N6 Regensburg
32D2 Reggane
20F5 Reggio di Calabria
20D2 Reggio nell'Emilia
21K1 Reghin
44H4 Regina
55B4 Registro
36C2 Rehoboth
48D3 Rehoboth Bay
15G7 Reigate
18G2 Reims
13M4 Reinbek
45H4 Reindeer Lake
19G6 Relizane
13L3 Rendsburg
16E5 Renfrew
54B4 Rengo
21M2 Reni
41I6 Renmark
18D2 Rennes
46D4 Reno
32C3 Réo
17E4 Republic of Ireland
36F5 Republic of South Africa
55A4 Reserva
54E3 Resistencia
21I2 Reșița
55C2 Resplendor
50F6 Retalhuleu
14G5 Retford
21K7 Rethymno
7 Réunion *terr.*
19G3 Reus
13L6 Reutlingen
50B5 Revillagigedo, Islas *is*
27H4 Rewa
46E3 Rexburg
10□1 Reykjavík
46H6 Reynosa
11O8 Rēzekne
13K4 Rheine
13K5 Rhine *r.*
18I2 Rhine *r.*
47J2 Rhinelander
20C2 Rho
48F2 Rhode Island *state*
21M6 Rhodes
21M6 Rhodes *i.*
21J4 Rhodope Mountains
18G5 Rhône *r.*
14D5 Rhyl
53I5 Riachão
55C1 Riacho de Santana
55C1 Riacho dos Machados
55A1 Rialma
49D3 Rialto
27J6 Riau, Kepulauan *is*
54F2 Ribas do Rio Pardo
14E5 Ribble *r.*
11F9 Ribe
55B3 Ribeirão Preto
52E6 Riberalta
23F7 Rîbnița
37K5 Richards Bay
46E4 Richfield
46D2 Richland
42E4 Richmond
47K4 Richmond
47K4 Richmond
48C4 Richmond
49A2 Richmond
47L3 Rideau Lakes
49D3 Ridgecrest
13N5 Riesa
11L9 Rietavas
20E3 Rieti
11N8 Rīga
11M8 Riga, Gulf of
11N6 Riihimäki
32D3 Rijau
20F2 Rijeka
31F5 Rikuzen-takata
21J3 Rila *mts*
18G4 Rillieux-la-Pape
13R6 Rimavská Sobota
20E2 Rimini
45L5 Rimouski
11F8 Ringkøbing
11G9 Ringsted
15F8 Ringwood
42B6 Ringwood
55A4 Rio Azul
52C4 Riobamba
55C3 Rio Bonito
52E6 Rio Branco
54F2 Rio Brilhante
55C3 Rio Casca
55B3 Rio Claro
54D4 Río Cuarto
55C1 Rio de Contas
55C3 Rio de Janeiro
55C3 Rio de Janeiro *state*
55A4 Rio do Sul
54C8 Río Gallegos
50D4 Río Grande
54C8 Río Grande
54F4 Rio Grande
46H6 Rio Grande *r.*
46H6 Rio Grande City
55A5 Rio Grande do Sul *state*
52D1 Ríohacha
52C5 Rioja
50G4 Río Lagartos
53K5 Rio Largo
18F4 Riom
55C3 Rio Novo
55C1 Rio Pardo de Minas
55C3 Rio Preto
46F4 Rio Rancho
55A2 Rio Verde
53H7 Rio Verde de Mato Grosso
23F6 Ripky
15F5 Ripley
14F4 Ripon
15D7 Risca
11F7 Risør
20D2 Riva del Garda
51G6 Rivas
54E4 Rivera
32C4 River Cess
48E2 Riverhead
49D4 Riverside
45L5 Riverview
45L5 Rivière-du-Loup
23E6 Rivne
35C5 Rivungo
34E1 Riyadh
23I8 Rize
15G6 Roade
51L5 Road Town
18G3 Roanne
48B4 Roanoke
47L4 Roanoke Rapids
48B2 Roaring Spring
51G5 Roatán
36D7 Robertson
32B4 Robertsport
45K5 Roberval
40D5 Robinson Range *hills*
41I6 Robinvale
54F4 Rocha
14E5 Rochdale
18D4 Rochefort
22I3 Rochegda
15H7 Rochester
42B6 Rochester
47I3 Rochester
48C1 Rochester
48F1 Rochester
15H7 Rochford
47J3 Rockford
41K4 Rockhampton
40D6 Rockingham
47I3 Rock Island
48F1 Rockland
48C3 Rockville
46F3 Rocky Mountains
55A4 Rodeio
18F4 Rodez
22I4 Rodniki
12I5 Roeselare
49A1 Rohnert Park
13N6 Rohrbach in Oberösterreich
11M8 Roja
54D4 Rojas
11N9 Rokiškis
23E6 Rokytne
55A3 Rolândia
52F6 Rolim de Moura
47I4 Rolla
21L1 Roman
21K2 Romania
18G4 Romans-sur-Isère
29E6 Romblon
20E4 Rome
47J5 Rome
48D1 Rome
15H7 Romford
18F2 Romilly-sur-Seine
23G6 Romny
23J5 Romodanovo
18E3 Romorantin-Lanthenay
15F8 Romsey
19D5 Ronda
54F2 Rondon
53H7 Rondonópolis
11I9 Rønne
11I8 Ronneby
12J5 Roosendaal
18D4 Roquefort
46D5 Rosario
50C4 Rosario
52D1 Rosario
53J4 Rosário
54D4 Rosario
54F4 Rosário do Sul
53G6 Rosário Oeste
18C2 Roscoff
17D4 Roscommon
17E5 Roscrea
51L5 Roseau
46C3 Roseburg
47H6 Rosenberg
13N7 Rosenheim
20F3 Roseto degli Abruzzi
44H4 Rosetown
49B1 Roseville
42F1 Rosewood
36C4 Rosh Pinah
20D3 Rosignano Marittimo
21K2 Roșiori de Vede
11H9 Roskilde
23G5 Roslavl'
20G5 Rossano
32B3 Rosso
15E7 Ross-on-Wye
23H6 Rossosh'
56B4 Ross Sea
13N3 Rostock
22H4 Rostov
23H7 Rostov-na-Donu
10L4 Rosvik
46G5 Roswell
13M6 Roth
14F5 Rotherham
43F4 Rotorua
12J5 Rotterdam
13L6 Rottweil
18F1 Roubaix
15I9 Rouen
16F1 Rousay *i.*
10N3 Rovaniemi
23H6 Roven'ki
20D2 Rovereto
20D2 Rovigo
20E2 Rovinj
23J6 Rovnoye
15G6 Royston
21N1 Rozdil'na
23I5 Rtishchevo
15D6 Ruabon
43F5 Ruahine Range *mts*
34E2 Rub' al Khālī *des.*
24J4 Rubtsovsk
13Q5 Ruda Śląska
23F5 Rudnya
23J6 Rudnya
26F1 Rudnyy
24G1 Rudol'fa, Ostrov *i.*
35D4 Rufiji *r.*
54D4 Rufino
32B3 Rufisque
15F6 Rugby
15F6 Rugeley
13N3 Rügen *i.*
34C4 Ruhengeri
55C1 Rui Barbosa
35D4 Ruipa
50C4 Ruiz
11N8 Rūjiena
35D4 Rukwa, Lake
16C4 Rum *i.*
21H2 Ruma
34E1 Rumāh
33F4 Rumbek
35D5 Rumphi
14E5 Runcorn
35B5 Rundu
35D5 Rusape
21K3 Ruse
15G6 Rushden
42B6 Rushworth
47I4 Russellville
13L5 Rüsselsheim
24I3 Russian Federation
23J5 Russkiy Kameshkir
23J8 Rust'avi
37H3 Rustenburg
47I5 Ruston
42C6 Rutherglen
15D5 Ruthin
48E1 Rutland
22H5 Ruza
23J5 Ruzayevka
13Q6 Ružomberok
34C4 Rwanda
16D5 Ryan, Loch *b.*
23H5 Ryazan'
23I5 Ryazhsk
22H4 Rybinsk
22H4 Rybinskoye Vodokhranilishche *resr*
13Q5 Rybnik
23H5 Rybnoye
15F8 Ryde
15H8 Rye
23G6 Ryl'sk
23K7 Ryn-Peski *des.*
31B8 Ryukyu Islands
23D6 Rzeszów
23I5 Rzhaksa
22G4 Rzhev

S

13M5 Saale *r.*
13M5 Saalfeld
13K6 Saarbrücken
11M7 Saaremaa *i.*
10N3 Saarenkylä
10N5 Saarijärvi
13K6 Saarlouis
21H2 Šabac
19H3 Sabadell
31E6 Sabae
55C2 Sabará
33E2 Sabhā
46G6 Sabinas
46G6 Sabinas Hidalgo
45L5 Sable, Cape
32D3 Sabon Kafi
26E3 Sabzevār
21K2 Săcele
31C6 Sach'on
48F1 Saco
49B1 Sacramento
55B2 Sacramento
49B1 Sacramento *r.*
46F5 Sacramento Mountains
37H7 Sada
19F2 Sádaba
34E2 Şa'dah
32B3 Sadiola
23J7 Sadovoye
11G8 Sæby
11H7 Säffle
46F5 Safford
15H6 Saffron Walden
32C1 Safi
23G5 Safonovo
23G8 Safranbolu
31C6 Saga
31E6 Sagami-nada *g.*
27G4 Sagar
47K3 Saginaw
47K3 Saginaw Bay
19B5 Sagres
47K7 Sagua la Grande
19D2 Sahagún
32D3 Sahara *des.*
32C3 Sahel *reg.*
50D4 Sahuayo
19G6 Saïda
31D6 Saijō
31C6 Saiki
11P6 Saimaa *l.*
15B8 St Agnes
15G7 St Albans
18F3 St-Amand-Montrond
16G4 St Andrews
51I5 St Ann's Bay
45M4 St Anthony
42A6 St Arnaud
47K6 St Augustine
15C8 St Austell
51L5 St-Barthélemy *i.*
14D4 St Bees Head
15B7 St Bride's Bay
18C2 St-Brieuc
48B1 St Catharines
18G4 St-Chamond
47I4 St Charles
48C3 St Charles
47K3 St Clair, Lake
18G3 St-Claude
15C7 St Clears
47I2 St Cloud
15B7 St David's Head
18H2 St-Dié
18G2 St-Dizier
44D3 St Elias Mountains
18D4 Saintes
18G4 St-Étienne
15I9 St-Étienne-du-Rouvray
18E5 St-Gaudens
42D2 St George
49F2 St George
51L6 St George's
17F6 St George's Channel
18I3 St Gotthard Pass
49A1 St Helena
6 St Helena and Dependencies *terr.*
14E5 St Helens
41J8 St Helens
46C2 St Helens, Mount *vol.*
15E9 St Helier
15B8 St Ives
15G6 St Ives
45K5 St-Jean, Lac *l.*
47M2 St-Jérôme
45L5 Saint John
45M5 St John's
51L5 St John's
47M3 St Johnsbury
47I4 St Joseph
15B8 St Just
12C2 St Kilda *is*
51L5 St Kitts and Nevis
53H2 St-Laurent-du-Maroni
45L5 St Lawrence *inlet*
45L5 St Lawrence, Gulf of
44B3 St Lawrence Island
18D2 St-Lô
32B3 St-Louis
47I4 St Louis
51L6 St Lucia
16□ St Magnus Bay
18C2 St-Malo
18C2 St-Malo, Golfe de *g.*
51J5 St-Marc
51L5 St-Martin *i.*
18D4 St-Médard-en-Jalles
18C3 St-Nazaire
15G6 St Neots
18H2 St-Nicolas-de-Port
18F1 St-Omer
47I3 St Paul
15E9 St Peter Port
11Q7 St Petersburg
47K6 St Petersburg
45M5 St-Pierre
45M5 St Pierre and Miquelon *terr.*
18F2 St-Quentin
48A1 St Thomas
18H5 St-Tropez
15F9 St-Vaast-la-Hougue
41H7 St Vincent, Gulf
51L6 St Vincent and the Grenadines
31D6 Sakaide
26D4 Sakākah
21L4 Sakar *mts*
21N4 Sakarya
32C4 Sakassou
31E5 Sakata
31B4 Sakchu
30F2 Sakhalin *i.*
30F2 Sakhalinskaya Oblast' *admin. div.*
30F1 Sakhalinskiy Zaliv *b.*
37I4 Sakhile
23J8 Şäki
11M9 Šakiai
29C6 Sakon Nakhon
31F6 Sakura
23G7 Saky
11J7 Sala
11N8 Salacgrīva
54E3 Saladas
26E5 Şalālah
19D3 Salamanca
50D4 Salamanca
11L8 Salantai
11N8 Salaspils
11N9 Šalčininkai
19D2 Saldaña
36C7 Saldanha
11M8 Saldus
42C7 Sale
24H3 Salekhard
27G5 Salem
46C3 Salem
48A2 Salem
48A4 Salem
48F1 Salem
20F4 Salerno
20F4 Salerno, Golfo di *g.*
14E5 Salford
13Q6 Salgótarján
53K5 Salgueiro
21M5 Salihli
11O10 Salihorsk
35D5 Salima
46H4 Salina
50E5 Salina Cruz
49B2 Salinas
50D4 Salinas
52B4 Salinas
55C2 Salinas
49B2 Salinas *r.*
53I4 Salinópolis
15F7 Salisbury
48D3 Salisbury
15E7 Salisbury Plain
22F3 Salmi
44G4 Salmon Arm
46D3 Salmon River Mountains
11M6 Salo
18G5 Salon-de-Provence
23I7 Sal'sk
54C2 Salta
15C8 Saltash
16E5 Saltcoats
46G6 Saltillo
46E3 Salt Lake City
54E4 Salto
55B3 Salto
49E4 Salton Sea *salt l.*
55D1 Salvador
34F1 Salwah
27I4 Salween *r.*
13N7 Salzburg
13M4 Salzgitter
29E6 Samar *i.*
23K5 Samara
29D8 Samarinda
26F3 Samarkand
33H1 Sāmarrā'
27H4 Sambalpur
35F5 Sambava
23D6 Sambir
54E5 Samborombón, Bahía *b.*
31C5 Samch'ŏk
34D4 Same
34E1 Samīrah
23J8 Şämkir
39I3 Samoa
20F2 Samobor
22I3 Samoded
21J3 Samokov
21L6 Samos *i.*
23I6 Samoylovka
29D8 Sampit
23H8 Samsun
32C3 San
34E2 Şan'ā'
33H1 Sanandaj
46G5 San Angelo
46H6 San Antonio
54B4 San Antonio
54D6 San Antonio Oeste
20E3 San Benedetto del Tronto
49D3 San Bernardino
54B4 San Bernardo
46G6 San Buenavetura
52E2 San Carlos
54B5 San Carlos
54B6 San Carlos de Bariloche
54D5 San Carlos de Bolívar
49D4 San Clemente
52D2 San Cristóbal
54D4 San Cristóbal
50F5 San Cristóbal de las Casas
51I4 Sancti Spíritus
29D7 Sandakan
21J4 Sandanski
16G1 Sanday *i.*
15E5 Sandbach
11G7 Sandefjord
49D4 San Diego
21N5 Sandıklı
11D7 Sandnes
10H3 Sandnessjøen
23D6 Sandomierz
20E2 San Donà di Piave
27I5 Sandoway
46D2 Sandpoint
10□2 Sandur
47K3 Sandusky
11G7 Sandvika
11J6 Sandviken
46E5 San Felipe
52E1 San Felipe
54B4 San Felipe
19C5 San Fernando
29E6 San Fernando
46H7 San Fernando
49C3 San Fernando
51L6 San Fernando
54B4 San Fernando
52E2 San Fernando de Apure
47K6 Sanford
47L4 Sanford
48F1 Sanford
49A2 San Francisco
54D4 San Francisco
49A2 San Francisco Bay *inlet*
19G4 San Francisco Javier
49C3 San Gabriel Mountains
25N3 Sangar
49C2 Sanger
20G5 San Giovanni in Fiore
29D7 Sangkulirang
27G5 Sangli
32E4 Sangmélima
46F4 Sangre de Cristo Range *mts*
52E6 San Ignacio
52F7 San Ignacio
49D4 San Jacinto
31E5 Sanjō
49B1 San Joaquin *r.*
49B2 San Joaquin Valley
54C7 San Jorge, Golfo de *g.*
29E6 San Jose
49B2 San Jose
51H7 San José
29E6 San Jose de Buenavista
46E6 San José de Comondú
52D3 San José del Guaviare
54E4 San José de Mayo
51K5 San Juan
54C4 San Juan
54E3 San Juan Bautista
52E2 San Juan de los Morros
46F4 San Juan Mountains
54D4 San Justo
18I3 Sankt Gallen
13O6 Sankt Pölten
13O7 Sankt Veit an der Glan
33G1 Şanlıurfa
52C3 San Lorenzo
54D4 San Lorenzo
19C5 Sanlúcar de Barrameda
50C4 San Lucas
49E4 San Luis
54C4 San Luis
49B3 San Luis Obispo
50D4 San Luis Potosí
46H6 San Marcos
20E3 San Marino
20E3 San Marino *country*
54C4 San Martín
54B6 San Martín de los Andes
49A2 San Mateo
54D6 San Matías, Golfo *g.*
50G6 San Miguel
54C3 San Miguel de Tucumán
55A1 San Miguel do Araguaia
32C4 Sanniquellie
23D6 Sanok
32C4 San-Pédro
54D2 San Pedro
49C4 San Pedro Channel
46G6 San Pedro de las Colonias
51K5 San Pedro de Macorís
54E2 San Pedro de Ycuamandyyú
50G5 San Pedro Sula
16F5 Sanquhar
49A2 San Rafael
54C4 San Rafael
20B3 San Remo
50G6 San Salvador
54C2 San Salvador de Jujuy
32D3 Sansanné-Mango
19E3 San Sebastián de los Reyes
20F4 San Severo
49D4 Santa Ana
50G6 Santa Ana
46F6 Santa Bárbara
49C3 Santa Barbara
55C2 Santa Bárbara
49B3 Santa Barbara Channel
55B3 Santa Bárbara d'Oeste
49D4 Santa Catalina, Gulf of
55A4 Santa Catarina *state*
49B2 Santa Clara
51I4 Santa Clara
49C3 Santa Clarita
49A2 Santa Cruz
52F7 Santa Cruz
53K5 Santa Cruz
55D2 Santa Cruz Cabrália
51I4 Santa Cruz del Sur
32B2 Santa Cruz de Tenerife
54F3 Santa Cruz do Sul
46F4 Santa Fe
54D4 Santa Fé
55A3 Santa Fé do Sul
53I4 Santa Helena
55A2 Santa Helena de Goiás
53I4 Santa Inês
32□ Santa Maria
49B3 Santa Maria
54F3 Santa Maria
55B1 Santa Maria da Vitória
55C2 Santa Maria do Suaçuí
55C3 Santa Maria Madalena
52D1 Santa Marta
49C3 Santa Monica
49C4 Santa Monica Bay
55C1 Santana
19E2 Santander
20C5 Sant'Antioco
53J4 Santa Quitéria
19B4 Santarém
53H4 Santarém
49A1 Santa Rosa
54D5 Santa Rosa
54F3 Santa Rosa
50G6 Santa Rosa de Copán
46E6 Santa Rosalía
55A2 Santa Vitória
49D4 Santee
51H7 Santiago
51J5 Santiago
54B4 Santiago
54F3 Santiago
19B2 Santiago de Compostela
51I4 Santiago de Cuba
54D3 Santiago del Estero
19G3 Sant Jordi, Golf de *g.*
55D1 Santo Amaro
55C3 Santo Amaro de Campos
55A3 Santo Anastácio
55B3 Santo André
54F3 Santo Angelo
32D4 Santo António
55A3 Santo Antônio da Platina
55D1 Santo Antônio de Jesus
52E4 Santo Antônio do Içá
51K5 Santo Domingo
55B3 Santos
55C3 Santos Dumont
54E3 Santo Tomé
50G6 San Vicente
52C6 San Vicente de Cañete
29C6 Sanya
55B3 São Bernardo do Campo
54E3 São Borja
55B3 São Carlos
55B1 São Domingos
53H5 São Félix
53H6 São Félix
55D1 São Félix
55C3 São Fidélis
55B1 São Francisco
55C1 São Francisco *r.*
55A5 São Francisco de Paula
55A4 São Francisco do Sul
54F4 São Gabriel
55C3 São Gonçalo
55B2 São Gonçalo do Abaeté
55B3 São Gonçalo do Sapucaí
55B2 São Gotardo
55C3 São João da Barra
55B3 São João da Boa Vista
19B3 São João da Madeira
55B1 São João da Ponte
55B3 São João del Rei
55C1 São João do Paraíso
55A5 São Joaquim
55B3 São Joaquim da Barra
55A4 São José
55A3 São José do Rio Preto
55B3 São José dos Campos
55A4 São José dos Pinhais
55A5 São Leopoldo
55B3 São Lourenço
53J4 São Luís
55A2 São Luís de Montes Belos
55A3 São Manuel
55D2 São Mateus
55A4 São Mateus do Sul
53J5 São Miguel do Tapuio
18G4 Saône *r.*
55B3 São Paulo
55A3 São Paulo *state*
52E4 São Paulo de Olivença
55C3 São Pedro da Aldeia
53J5 São Raimundo Nonato
55B2 São Romão
55B3 São Roque
55B3 São Sebastião
55B3 São Sebastião do Paraíso
53H7 São Simão
55B3 São Simão
32D4 São Tomé
32D4 São Tomé and Príncipe
55B3 São Vicente
21N4 Sapanca
32C3 Sapouy
23I5 Sapozhok
30F4 Sapporo
33H1 Saqqez
29C6 Sara Buri
20H3 Sarajevo
24G4 Saraktash
23J5 Saransk
24G4 Sarapul
47K6 Sarasota
21M1 Sarata
46F3 Saratoga
49A2 Saratoga
23J6 Saratov
23J5 Saratovskoye Vodokhranilishche *resr*
26F4 Saravan
21L4 Saray
21M6 Sarayköy
20C4 Sardinia *i.*
26F3 Sar-e Pol
27G3 Sargodha
33E4 Sarh
26E3 Sārī
21M5 Sarıgöl
41J4 Sarina
33E2 Sarīr Tibesti *des.*
31B5 Sariwŏn
21M4 Sarıyer
27G2 Sarkand
21N5 Şarkikaraağaç
21L4 Şarköy
18I3 Sarnen
47K3 Sarnia
23E6 Sarny
21L4 Saros Körfezi *b.*
23I5 Sarova
11G7 Sarpsborg
18H2 Sarrebourg
20G1 Sárvár
31C6 Sasebo
44H4 Saskatchewan *prov.*
44H4 Saskatchewan *r.*
44H4 Saskatoon
37H4 Sasolburg
23I5 Sasovo
32C4 Sassandra
20C4 Sassari
13N3 Sassnitz
27G4 Satpura Range *mts*
23D7 Satu Mare
46F6 Saucillo
11E71[2] Sauðárkrókur
26D4 Saudi Arabia
45J5 Sault Sainte Marie
47K2 Sault Sainte Marie
26F1 Saumalkol'
18D3 Saumur
35C4 Saurimo
20I2 Sava *r.*
32D4 Savalou
47K5 Savannah
47K5 Savannah *r.*
29C6 Savannakhét
51I5 Savanna-la-Mar
10L5 Sävar
21L5 Savaștepe
20C2 Savona
10P6 Savonlinna
11I8 Sävsjö
33G2 Sawhāj
42F3 Sawtell
40E1 Sawu, Laut *sea*
14G5 Saxilby
15I6 Saxmundham
32D3 Say
34F2 Sayḩūt
27K2 Saynshand
48D2 Sayreville
16F2 Scapa Flow *inlet*
14G4 Scarborough
45K5 Scarborough
51L6 Scarborough
18I3 Schaffhausen
13N6 Schärding
48E1 Schenectady
20D2 Schio
13L3 Schleswig
13M4 Schönebeck (Elbe)
13L7 Schwäbische Alb *mts*
13L6 Schwäbisch Hall
13N6 Schwandorf
13N5 Schwarzenberg
13M7 Schwaz
13O4 Schwedt an der Oder
13M5 Schweinfurt
13M4 Schwerin
18I3 Schwyz
20E6 Sciacca
20F6 Scicli
16F4 Scone
42E4 Scone
16F3 Scotland *admin. div.*
46G3 Scottsbluff
47J5 Scottsboro
48D2 Scranton
14G5 Scunthorpe
21H3 Scutari, Lake
15H8 Seaford
14G4 Seamer
47I4 Searcy
46C2 Seattle
32D3 Sebba
21J2 Sebeș
11P8 Sebezh
47K6 Sebring
44F5 Sechelt
52B5 Sechura
37I4 Secunda
27G5 Secunderabad
47I4 Sedalia
18G2 Sedan
20B6 Sédrata
11M9 Šeduva
32B4 Sefadu
37H2 Sefare
21L5 Seferihisar
27J6 Segamat
22G3 Segezha
32C3 Ségou
19D3 Segovia
32C4 Séguéla
46H6 Seguin
10M5 Seinäjoki
15H9 Seine *r.*
15G9 Seine, Baie de *b.*
18F2 Seine, Val de *valley*
11M9 Sejny
29C8 Sekayu
32C4 Sekondi
34D2 Sek'ot'a
14F5 Selby
35C6 Selebi-Phikwe
21M5 Selendi
32B3 Sélibabi
22G4 Selizharovo
16G5 Selkirk
45I4 Selkirk
44G4 Selkirk Mountains
47J5 Selma
49C2 Selma
23G5 Sel'tso
22L4 Selty
52D5 Selvas *reg.*
44E3 Selwyn Mountains
29D8 Semarang